Praise for *I ♥ Me* :

'I knew I was going to like Dr David Hamilton the first time I met him at an I Can Do It! conference in London. Not only does he regularly engage in victory dancing, one of my all-time favourite activities, but he's a pedigreed scientist with actual evidence that kindness, striking poses and loving yourself is good for the planet. Plus, his story about Dove deodorant falling from the sky is one of my all-time favorite manifestation stories. I was lucky enough to preview an early copy of this wise and wonderful book. And I have but one thing to say: "Why is this not required reading? Why is this not the first book we're handed in life?" It definitely should be.'

PAM GROUT, AUTHOR OF 17 BOOKS INCLUDING *NY TIMES* BESTSELLING *E-SQUARED* AND *E-CUBED*

'Give yourself the gift of self-love and read this inspiring book.'

ROBERT HOLDEN PHD, AUTHOR OF *SHIFT HAPPENS!* AND *LOVEABILITY*

'Feeling unable to be kind to ourselves is an issue for so many - and often the cause of our physical and emotional health issues. David's wise, personal and practical guide to regaining our innate ability to experience self-compassion is such a gift for anyone wanting to move their life and health onwards. I love it.'

PHIL PARKER, EXPERT IN THE PSYCHOLOGY OF HEALTH, HAPPINESS AND GENIUS, INVENTOR OF THE LIGHTNING PROCESS®

'David's beautiful book has been written from his heart and holds within it the power to return you to yours. Just like David, the guidance shared is genuine, honest and real, and if you want to learn how to love yourself more then I wholeheartedly recommend reading his wise words.'

SANDY C. NEWBIGGING, BESTSELLING AUTHOR OF *MIND CALM*

'David has lived every step of this book, which is packed with illuminating science, warm anecdotes and easy-to-apply techniques. His heart and soul shine through every page and the world will be richer for it.'
ANDREA GARDNER, AUTHOR OF CHANGE YOUR WORDS, CHANGE YOUR WORLD

'I LOVE this book, and especially how David weaves science, personal insights and practical ways to feel good about yourself with such an open heart. Get ready to feel nourished and uplifted as you embark upon a wonderful journey of self-love and healing.'
ALISOUN MACKENZIE, AUTHOR OF HEARTATUDE: THE 9 PRINCIPLES OF HEART-CENTERED SUCCESS

'The greatest gift you can give the world is to be at peace with yourself, and self-love is fundamental to that peace. David's book is a wonderful contribution to understanding how you can release learned emotional patterns and allow your natural self-love and compassion to surface. Read it to be inspired, moved and transformed. Thank you, David.'
NICK WILLIAMS, BESTSELLING AUTHOR OF THE WORK WE WERE BORN TO DO

THE SCIENCE OF SELF-LOVE

DAVID R. HAMILTON PhD

HAY HOUSE

Carlsbad, California • New York City
London • Sydney • New Delhi

Published in the United Kingdom by:
Hay House UK Ltd, The Sixth Floor, Watson House,
54 Baker Street, London W1U 7BU
Tel: +44 (0)20 3927 7290; Fax: +44 (0)20 3927 7291; www.hayhouse.co.uk

Published in the United States of America by:
Hay House Inc., PO Box 5100, Carlsbad, CA 92018-5100
Tel: (1) 760 431 7695 or (800) 654 5126
Fax: (1) 760 431 6948 or (800) 650 5115; www.hayhouse.com

Published in Australia by:
Hay House Australia Ltd, 18/36 Ralph St, Alexandria NSW 2015
Tel: (61) 2 9669 4299; Fax: (61) 2 9669 4144; www.hayhouse.com.au

Published in India by:
Hay House Publishers India, Muskaan Complex, Plot No.3, B-2,
Vasant Kunj, New Delhi 110 070
Tel: (91) 11 4176 1620; Fax: (91) 11 4176 1630; www.hayhouse.co.in

Text © David Hamilton, 2015

The moral rights of the author have been asserted.

The information given in this book should not be treated as a substitute for
professional medical advice; always consult a medical practitioner. Any use of
information in this book is at the reader's discretion and risk. Neither the author nor
the publisher can be held responsible for any loss, claim or damage arising out of
the use, or misuse, of the suggestions made, the failure to take medical advice or for
any material on third party websites.

A catalogue record for this book is available from the British Library.

ISBN: 978-1-78180-184-0

Printed and bound by CPI Group (UK) Ltd, Croydon, CR0 4YY

To Oscar

Contents

List of Exercises

Foreword

Self-love is something very close to my own heart. In fact, you could say that self-love saved my life.

I had a Near Death Experience (NDE) in 2006. I had been very sick with cancer – it was stage 4 lymphoma, and had spread throughout my body and had metastasized. I had tumors, many of them the size of lemons, from the base of my skull, all around my neck, under my arms, my breasts, and in my abdomen. My body stopped absorbing nourishment and went into catabolisys. My lungs were perpetually filled with fluid that needed to be drained regularly, and I was connected to piped oxygen.

Then on February 2nd, 2006, I fell into a deep coma. The doctors told my family that my body had gone into organ failure and that I was now in my final hours of life.

But while my body was close to death, I was very much alive. I felt myself as separate from my body, and I felt incredible! My family were gathered all around my weak and dying physical body, and had no idea that I could see them all. At one point I felt myself expand, so much in fact that I felt myself to be the whole universe as a state of consciousness. Among many things

I felt and understood during this experience, one thing was immediately relevant to my life.

I understood that cancer in my body was a manifestation of my own energy that had turned inwards on itself. This is not to say that such a thing is true for anybody else as we are all unique in our own ways. But I had very little self-love. I had lived most of my life on other people's terms. I was not living as my true authentic self.

I understood that if I chose to love myself, uninhibited, unreservedly, to express my authentic self from that moment onwards, then I would recover from cancer. I also understood that self-love was the most important thing that we humans need to learn and that, sadly, most people simply don't know how.

This is one of the reasons why I love this book by David Hamilton. He decided to tackle the subject after a conversation we shared, along with my husband Danny, a few years ago. In this book he is open about his own self-love journey and honest about the many times when he seemed to be lacking in it. He has shared some of his personal struggles and I am certain that many readers will be able to relate to them because all of us are, after all, human and we share in many of the same kinds of difficulties that grow out of a lack of self-love.

David has approached the subject in multiple ways, thereby offering something to just about anyone who struggles with their self-esteem. Being a former scientist, he brings a brand new approach to self-love that breakthroughs in neuroscience have made possible. He shows how self-love can be wired into the brain and he shares some science in the simplest possible way on how we can actually achieve this for ourselves.

We also learn that we are not born devoid of self-love. In fact, babies and young children exude it. A self-love deficit, as David sometimes refers to the feeling of low self-love, is something we learn through life. And as David points out, learning distils down to the formation of brain connections so this also means that a lack of self-love can actually be unlearned, and a healthy sense of self-love learned in its place and laid down into the brain's neural architecture.

He also discusses the importance of being authentic and letting our guard down, having the courage to show our vulnerabilities, and he even teaches us how we can develop resilience to shame, which many people struggle with. In one chapter, we can even learn how to be more gentle and compassionate towards ourselves.

Towards the end of the book, I like that David describes, scientifically, how we are made of love, that we are all indeed beings of light, and shares the most remarkable personal story that he calls the 'Dove Miracle' that happened through this insightful blend of science and spirit. As beings of light, he encourages us to step up, be our authentic selves, and own our worth.

What makes this such an authentic book on self-love is that David has lived through a self-love deficit himself for most of his life. As he writes in the Introduction, it took him much longer to write it than he expected and this is because he had to learn how to love himself first.

He speaks from experience and I am sure you will be able to learn from his experience and gain from his insights, wisdom, and encouragement and from many of the exercises within the book.

I hope you come to love and appreciate David's important work as much as I have!

Anita Moorjani

New York Times bestselling author of *Dying to be Me: My Journey from Cancer to Near Death to True Healing*

Acknowledgements

Writing this book has been a real journey for me. I believe that Oscar, my two-year-old Labrador, arrived in my life to help me with it. Without his love, his example, the daily laughter he produces and the call to be his guardian, I wouldn't have been able to change enough to complete the book. For a significant personal change is what this book has required.

My partner, Elizabeth Caproni, has accompanied me on this journey and I am deeply grateful for her love, her companionship and her patience with me as I stuttered and stammered towards a different way of looking at myself, my life and my place in the world. I am also grateful to Elizabeth for finding important research statistics that add value to the book, and for the many helpful suggestions she made throughout the writing process, including allowing me to use her poem in Chapter 7.

I will be eternally grateful to Robert Holden for his friendship and support. Throughout the writing of this book Robert has been a constant source of friendship, support and inspiration. I could fill a book with the notes about life, love and the universe that I scribbled down on random bits of paper, napkins, coffee cups, the back of my hand or whatever else I could find when Robert called to ask how the book was coming along – and of course to enquire about Elizabeth, and Oscar's antics too.

One of my inspirations for this book has been Alyx Mia Redford. When I saw her kissing her own reflection in our full-length mirror and then giving herself a hug, I knew that this young lady had a lot to teach me about self-love. I've also been inspired by how her parents, my dear friends Bryce and Allyson, have guided her to remember that she is most definitely *enough*.

I am also grateful to Bryce for reading the manuscript of this book and offering me his insights, some of which helped shape the content.

To my dear friend Assad Negyal, thank you for being so thorough and offering such detailed feedback and so many valuable suggestions, many of which have formed some of the key sections of the book. And thank you for sharing some of your own vulnerabilities and for helping me realize how helpful this book could be.

And to Bhavna Patel, Gillian Sneddon and Margaret McCathie, thank you also for taking the time to read the manuscript and offering kind and honest feedback. Without your input, this book would be missing some vital insights.

I am indebted to Michelle Pilley, managing director of Hay House UK, for giving me the time I needed to write this book.

I am also grateful to everyone in the Hay House UK office. Even though we authors don't get to see and learn of all the contributions you make to our books, please know that I am deeply grateful for all that's done behind the scenes, from giving simple opinions and feedback on content to designing our books, making sure they are available and reach their UK and international audiences, supporting us in sales and marketing, ensuring that we have a presence in the digital world … I could go on.

And to my editor, Lizzie Henry, what can I say to express what a stellar job you've done in helping to shape this book into its final form? To me, you are worth your weight in gold.

Thanks also to Lizzie Prior for first pressing me on the importance of using the solid red heart logo on the cover, and creating a mock-cover for me to see.

I would also like to say some words of thanks to Anita Moorjani and her husband, Danny. It was our conversation after an 'I Can Do It' conference that inspired me to write this book and embark on my own self-love project.

Last, but certainly not least, I would like to say a heartfelt thank you to my parents, Robert and Janet Hamilton. You have always supported me, believed in me and encouraged me to be what I wanted to be. Your love, support, insights and parenting, even in my adult years, have helped me reach a space in my life where I can now say 'I *am* enough.'

Introduction

The first version of this book was rejected by my publisher. They'd wholeheartedly accepted my previous seven books. What was different about this one?

There were two reasons. First, as I point out in the first chapter, there are three stages of self-love. Many adults find themselves at the stage of 'I'm *not* enough.' Not good enough, not important enough, not successful enough… Most of us live out most of our life there, usually without realizing.

I didn't realize it myself until I was standing at the side of the stage at an 'I Can Do It' conference organized by my publisher. Dr Wayne Dyer, the internationally known author, speaker and 'father of motivation', was receiving a well-earned standing ovation following his talk. I was due to speak next.

It was September 2012 and a home gig for me. It was also the first time such a large self-help conference had come to Scotland. In the audience were a lot of people who were there to support me, including family, friends and people who had attended some of my other talks and workshops.

I should have been excited, but I wasn't. Everyone gets a little nervous before public speaking. That's normal. But what I experienced over the next few moments was more than nerves. It was a deep and profound sense of '*I'm not good enough.*'

I felt really small, insecure and basically unworthy – and the feeling was familiar. It took me back to when I was six years old and was being made to stand in the corner of the classroom because I hadn't brought 5p for a school trip. My teacher was saying, 'If David Hamilton isn't good enough to bring his money, we'll go on the trip without him.'

The rest of the class stood in line to collect a big yellow badge. I don't remember the details of it exactly, but I do remember it was large, bright and yellow. What it meant was that you were special. Clearly, everyone in the class was special. Standing in the corner, clearly I was not.

My mum would have given me the money without hesitation. But I hadn't asked her for it. I knew my mum and dad were struggling with money. A man used to visit us on Friday evenings and my mum would give him money, which he would note down in his big book. He was from the Provident. It was a company that offered loans to people who were in need. Tony was a nice man and he visited us every week for years. But one night close to Christmas time when I sneaked downstairs I saw Mum crying. She was explaining to Dad that my sister Lesley needed new clothes and that we both wanted specific toys for Christmas. She was saying, 'What am I going to do?'

I went back upstairs and cried too, half out of sympathy for my mum and half out of shame at being so selfish. I always spent all my pocket money on myself, but my mum never spent money on herself. Everything was for the family.

As a young child, you don't understand the value of money. Five pence could have been a week's wages for all I knew. That's why I hadn't asked Mum for the money.

Back at the conference, Wayne Dyer wasn't actually wearing a yellow badge, but he might as well have been. To my mind, all the other speakers were special. And I *wasn't*. I was just a guy from the wee village of Banknock. 'Who d'you think *you* are to be speaking at this conference?' said a voice in my head. 'Get back home to where you belong and leave the speaking to the big boys.'

Of course I couldn't go back home; I had to go on stage. Within a few moments, I was out there doing what I do best. No one would have guessed what I'd been feeling.

But those few moments were the first signs that I needed to address my personal issues. It wasn't the first time I'd felt small and insecure and it certainly wouldn't be the last. But now I knew I couldn't let it hold my life or career back any more than it already had done.

During Wayne Dyer's talk, he'd invited Anita Moorjani, bestselling author of the book *Dying to Be Me*, onto the stage to tell her story of having a near-death experience while suffering from stage-four lymphoma. Anita had experienced such a profound expansiveness that she'd felt herself to be the whole universe as a state of consciousness. In that state, she'd understood that learning to love ourselves was about the most important thing we could ever do and that most of us just didn't know how.

In London the following week I had the chance to spend a long time talking to Anita and her husband, Danny. Anita talked much more about self-love then and told me how she'd chosen to love herself completely and be her authentic self. And how she'd become free of cancer in a matter of a few months.

Meeting and conversing with Anita was like a clarion call to me. I realized that the root of almost all of my problems in life, especially the issue of confidence, was self-love. Never before had I been so sure of what to write my next book on. Writing a book on the subject was the only way I felt I could immerse myself in it enough to really experience self-love. So my self-love project began…

The book took much longer than I expected. This was linked to the second reason why it was different: I had a deadline to write it.

There are really only two kinds of self-help books. There's the type where a person has lived a philosophy and a set of teachings for several years and is now sharing their wisdom. Then there's the type where the content mirrors the author's life – where the writer learns as they write. This book falls into that category. Working on it has been, as I said, quite a personal journey for me. I've packed more growth into the last 21 months than the previous 10 years. My dog, Oscar, has helped me a lot.

Animals know all about self-love. They don't have a problem with it. Oscar came into my life as an eight-week-old Labrador puppy just as I was about to begin work on this book. It's funny how the timing of these things works out.

One of the things Oscar has inspired me to learn is that self-love doesn't mean 'love yourself *instead of* others'. Nor does it mean 'love yourself *once you've finished* loving others'. It doesn't even mean 'love yourself *as well as* others'. Others aren't mentioned *at all*. Love yourself. It's that simple.

In practice … well, it's not always that simple. The problem with having a deadline to write a book, especially one about self-love, is that it's like saying, 'You will love yourself by 30 June 2013.' That was my initial deadline.

Self-love doesn't work like that. You can't rush it. Having a deadline to love yourself ensures you'll never get there, because rushing the process is continually reinforcing 'I'm *not* good enough.' If you *were* good enough, you wouldn't be trying so hard to *be* good enough, right?

The managing director of my publisher removed my deadline. She asked me to come back to her when I felt I could finish the book. I'm very grateful she did that. It has allowed me to create a book of which I'm now very proud.

In this book you'll learn about the three stages of self-love and a possible fourth. You'll find out how a lack of self-love is learned. You weren't born that way. You learned it somewhere along the line, most likely in the first six or seven years of your life. Then, over time, it became normal for you. It was wired into your brain.

Part of this book is about teaching you how to wire in more positive beliefs instead. You'll get the chance to try lots of different exercises that will help you do that, some of which will literally alter your brain networks.

You'll also learn about shame and how to become resilient to it. And I'll encourage you to let your guard down. Don't be afraid to show your vulnerabilities. Everyone feels vulnerable, even people who pretend they're tough. Showing your vulnerabilities gives others permission to show theirs too. That's how friendships begin. Also, being yourself, without hiding or pretending in any way, is a back door to self-love.

You'll also learn how to be compassionate towards yourself and how to forgive yourself. That can be quite a stumbling block for some people. If it's one for you, then here are some insights and strategies for finally moving on in your life.

You'll also gain some insights that will help you to step up and out into the world, no longer afraid of being who or what you want to be.

A lot of what I've written is backed up by science. I'm a former pharmaceutical drug development scientist and I love to use science to inspire. As for what qualifies me to write a book about self-love – well, I'm human.

Just about every person I've ever known has struggled to some extent with self-love. Life doesn't seem to spare anyone from facing doubts about their own worth. We all tend to have the same kind of troubles. So you'll be able to recognize yourself in some of the personal stories and examples given throughout the book.

I've used the terms 'self-love', 'self-worth' and 'self-esteem' interchangeably for the most part. Although they're slightly different, most people tend to use them to describe the same thing – their own sense of worth and how it relates to their emotions and the circumstances of their life. Where I have used the terms more specifically, I've made it clear how they differ.

Overall, the book is packed with tools, tips, exercises, encouragement, inspiration and stories. My hope is that by the time you finish reading it, you'll love yourself enough to have already begun living the life you want to live.

Welcome to your own self-love project. Take your time … and enjoy the journey!

Part I

Where Are You Now?

'I don't want to earn my living. I want to live.'

OSCAR WILDE

Chapter 1

The Three Stages of Self-Love

*'The key to growth is the introduction
of higher dimensions of consciousness
into our awareness.'*

Lao Tzu

Most people spend most of their time in a state of consciousness that says, 'I'm *not* good enough' – or, more simply, 'I'm *not* enough.' Many people spend their entire life there. Some do a good job of pretending otherwise, but they're there just the same.

Others reach a point where they say, 'I've *had* enough!' It's a transition point. It's usually accompanied by passion and sometimes by anger, especially if these people feel they've been taken advantage of or bullied. Despite this, it's a much better place to be in than 'I'm *not* enough,' mostly because these people are less likely to be taken advantage of or bullied ever again.

In time, a lucky few pop out of the other end. They've had enough of having had enough. It's tiring because it takes quite a lot of energy to channel your mind in that way all the time. The lucky few emerge into a quite restful state, a state of 'I *am* good enough' or 'I *am* enough.' It's characterized by acceptance and peace, and a lot of laughter is not uncommon. Life ceases to be stressful, for the most part. Challenges still come along of course. Challenges are part of being human. But in this state we don't waste energy trying to maintain a charade or to get people to like or accept us. And it turns out that's quite a lot of saving on energy for most of us.

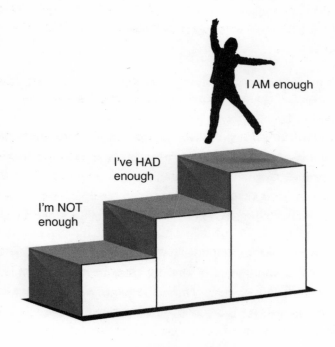

The three stages of self-love

Let's look at the three stages in more detail.

Stage 1: 'I'm *Not* Enough'

What qualifies me to write this book is that I spent most of the first 42 years of my life living in this state. Given you're reading this book, I'm guessing you spend a fair amount of time in it too.

This self-love deficit, as I sometimes refer to it, probably isn't at the forefront of your mind. You know it's there on some level, but it doesn't hang around for long in your daily waking consciousness. It's more like a cloaked goblin hiding behind a curtain in the recesses of your mind, ready to leap out and run the show whenever something potentially good looks to be on the horizon.

What's more, the world quite often reflects back to you your own feelings about yourself, usually in how people treat you.

I was bullied at school. It was never physical, more emotional. For years it was just teasing, but it came to a head in my sixth (final) year at high school, when I was 17 years old. The 'in-crowd', who accounted for about a fifth of the 60 or so people in the year, ran what resembled a campaign throughout the year.

It was cyber bullying in the days preceding the internet. They put up numerous posters around the school making fun of me. One day, for instance, was declared 'National "We Love Hammy" Day'. Hammy was my nickname, after Hamilton. There was little love on my day, but there was a lot of laughter.

Once, when the bullies were drunk (this occasionally happened, especially when they turned 18, and as sixth-year students we had our own common room), they tried to throw a bucket of water over me. As I approached the common room, one of the girls saw me coming and then ran excitedly into the room, so I knew something was about to happen. I considered turning around and walking away, but my bag was in there with my books in it and I needed them because it was close to exam time.

I felt nervous as I opened the common-room door. There was one boy standing on a chair, making an attempt to lasso me with a rope. He would probably have succeeded were it not for the fact that he was drunk. So I was able to catch the lasso and hold the rope. In the flurry of activity that happened next, the bucket of water was thrown at me but I was able to step aside and only soak up a few splashes on my trousers and shoes. It probably helped that I was the only person not drunk.

I picked up my bag from the table where I'd left it. Some of my friends were sitting there, but no one said a word. I left the room, bag in hand, and tried to find somewhere I could have a cry.

I felt like crying a lot of the time at school. Either that or I was anxious. I just accepted that that was the way life was. There didn't seem to be anything I could do to change it. When I'd plucked up the courage to ask one boy why they treated me the way they did, it had been met with a shocked, 'What are you talking about? How dare you!' Those weren't the exact words he used, but it was the sentiment. 'This is how it is, Hammy.'

The point was, his words resonated with what I felt was the truth about myself. Deep down I had the sense that, no matter what, I *wasn't good enough*.

I wouldn't admit to it, of course. I used to say that I was bullied because I was good at things. Even in the first draft of this book I wrote that. I also wrote that I learned to play myself down to avoid being targeted. In actual fact, I was bullied because I made a point of telling everyone that I was good at things. It wasn't because I was the fastest runner and had won a few trophies, or one of the cleverest students in the school, or that I did karate and had won a trophy for that too, or even that I could do all sorts of stunts on my BMX bike, including a wheelie for almost half a mile and jumping the bike over eight beer barrels at speed. It wasn't even the fact that some of the most popular and attractive girls in the year thought that I was good-looking. It was the fact that I repeatedly told people about my achievements.

Why was I doing it? It was because deep down I believed that I needed to keep giving people reasons to like me. If I stopped, they'd lose interest. And I was scared of being left out, shunned … alone.

When you feel you're *not* enough, it makes it easier for people to take advantage of you. You give off hidden signals, according to the science of victimology.

A group of prison inmates convicted of assault were asked to view videos of people walking along a busy sidewalk in New York City. Then they were asked which of those people they would target to assault or mug. Within seconds, they'd made their selections.

Most people would assume that the victims would be chosen according to size, but the criminals selected some large men and ignored some petite women. Their choice didn't turn out to have much to do with age, race or gender either. It was the way the passers-by held and moved their body that mattered the most. People whose body language conveyed uncertainty or little confidence – that is, *a feeling of not being good enough* – were almost always the ones targeted. Those who showed more self-confidence were largely ignored.[1]

Of course, this absolutely does *not* mean that people who have been bullied or abused or mugged have somehow brought it on themselves. Many attacks are completely random, plus bullies and abusers merely select someone they believe they can dominate, in order to compensate for their own self-love deficit.

But we all give off all sorts of signals. I'll look at some of them later in this book and, importantly, how to change them.

Stage 2: 'I've *Had* Enough'

Quite quickly as you set out on your journey to self-love, you reach the space where you've *had* enough. You've had enough of feeling inferior. You've had enough of being passed over for promotion. You've had enough of being bullied or taken advantage of. You've had enough of feeling small. You've had enough of feeling scared. You've had enough of having no confidence. You've had enough of giving your power away. I could go on. Let's just say you've *had enough*.

This is the place where wee miracles can happen, subtle shifts in the people or environment around you that just weren't happening before.

Once, early in my career as a writer and speaker, I was giving a talk to a group of schoolteachers. It was an in-service training day, where teachers get a day away from teaching and hear talks and receive training. The assistant head of this particular school had invited me to speak after attending one of my lectures a few months earlier. I was to deliver a one-hour talk that fused science with inspiration.

I often start this kind of talk with a few examples of the placebo effect, both to introduce my story of working in the pharmaceutical industry and becoming fascinated by the placebo effect and to introduce the concept that the mind is more powerful than we think. But this time, as I addressed the 100 or so teachers and administrative staff ranged in front of me, the bullying began.

A biology teacher spoke up first, stating, with a hint of aggression in his tone, that the placebo effect wasn't real, that there was no mind–body effect and that some people just got better. That was it.

Despite the fact that at the time I was probably one of the UK's foremost experts on the placebo effect, had written several chapters and articles on it, had delivered about 500 lectures on the mind–body connection, was consulted by TV production companies and had been invited to present a prime-time documentary on the subject, had a PhD and had worked as a scientist, learning, first-hand, how a person's expectation of recovery affected the outcome, the only words I could find in reply were: 'Oh, I've never thought of it like that. You might be right.'

I was scared. He was aggressive. I was no longer an adult; I was a child being spoken to by a stern schoolteacher.

My voice changed. I spoke more quietly. It wasn't intentional – my throat was constricted. I was now afraid of everyone in the lecture theatre.

And it got progressively worse. I was soon unable to say more than a few words without someone answering back. All I could do to stop from crying and embarrassing myself in front of a room full of adults was to breathe deeply and slow my speech right down.

It's funny what people see. Afterwards, the headmaster invited me into his office. He asked how I'd been able to refrain from getting angry and raising my voice. He thought my self-control was astonishing, a deeply inspiring lesson for everyone in the room, one that he would remember for a very long time. He applauded how I'd slowed my speech and taken deep breaths to control my emotions. He wanted to know how I'd done it, because he wanted to learn.

Of course, I didn't admit that there had come a point, about half an hour into the lecture, when I really was about to cry. I just couldn't take it any more. There were about five bullies who were speaking more than I was. Every sentence I uttered was met with attack. Then I had a strange moment of insight and clarity. I didn't actually *need* to stay there – I could just *walk away*. I was barely being paid anyway, once I'd covered my expenses. I was really doing this as a favour to the assistant head.

I suddenly felt an inner strength that was more relief than anything else. My parting gift would be a few choice words of my own.

The lectern was behind me. I had some notes on it and a bottle of water. I turned my back on my audience and picked them up. When I turned back around, I was going to tell them precisely where they could stick their in-service training. I'd *had* enough!

But just as I was about to speak, a young Australian girl stood up. She was in one of the front rows, over to my right.

'Dr Hamilton,' she said, 'can I just say how embarrassed I am to be in this audience right now. This is schoolyard bullying and these teachers should know better. I'm a student teacher from Australia, here for a year to gain experience. I can tell you now that this kind of behaviour would never happen in Australia. I want you to know that I am not part of this.'

There was a burst of applause. It was incredible. I felt washed with gratitude and relief.

When the applause ended, the teacher who was the ringleader of the bullies got up, shouted that he could give the same talk 'with a cross around my bloody neck' and stormed out of the door. The other four were without their leader.

People can behave out of character when they're in a group, especially if the group is a bullying one. Some people (and I count the remaining four teachers in this) have such low self-worth that they'll do almost anything to be accepted, including be mean and unkind. We're all driven by a need to belong.

Now their figurehead was gone, the four teachers were the most agreeable people in the room. They hung on my every word, leaning forward and nodding furiously. I could have said anything. I could have professed that the world was flat and these intelligent men would have seen my point.

Now I have real compassion for them because I see how much they wanted to make up for their earlier behaviour. I see them through the eyes of a person who can spot low self-worth. People who bully, dominate or control others have some of the lowest. Why else do you think they need to dominate? When they do, their secret feelings of *not enough* are temporarily replaced with *enough*.

Some people bully, too, because they're frustrated by their life, work or relationships. They dreamed of doing other things and weren't able to do them. Dominating others is the only sense of control they have. In those fleeting moments, the feeling of being *enough* acts as a sticking plaster over the wound of their low self-esteem.

Several years ago, my friend Ailsa and I were talking about self-help books. This was in the days before I had written any books at all. She was at the point of self-help fatigue, tired of constantly viewing the problems in her life as manifestations of her thoughts and emotions.

I shared a metaphor I was working on, one that I later included in *Is Your Life Mapped Out?* 'Life,' I suggested, 'is a bit like being in a small canoe on a wide river. Our mind is like an oar. We can use it to paddle left or right, forwards or backwards, or even do what many people do and paddle around in a wee circle. The river also has a current and sometimes, through no conscious choice or fault of our own, that current pulls us to the left or right, towards people, environments and circumstances.'

'Ha!' said Ailsa. 'It's OK for people who write self-help books and how-to-get-what-you-want-type books. Their rivers are calm. Me, I'm always in the rapids! And if one more person tells me to look within, I'm going to punch them!'

She always was the peacemaker.

Ailsa had *had* enough!

As I mentioned earlier, this stage is often characterized by passion and sometimes by bursts of anger. When we've *had* enough, we've had enough of things being the way they've been. We've had enough of feeling the way we've been feeling. We're going to step up and take control of our own life. And if anyone has a problem with that, tough!

This is why this is quite a healthy space to be in. At this point, we no longer feel that we have no control over our life. Even though we may not like our current circumstances, we realize that the one thing we do have control over is ourselves, and once we start exerting that control, we realize that we have more power to shape our personal reality than we thought.

This is the space where decisions are made, relationships are formed, strengthened or broken, promotions are obtained, new jobs sought, new respect found. This is the place where we decide to make changes to how and where we live. This is the place where we start to feel free.

Stage 3: 'I *Am* Enough'

Given enough time, many of us reach the stage of 'I *am* enough.' It's where we no longer have any need to show the world that we're the master of our own life. We feel it inside.

At this stage we don't feel any need to prove our worth, we don't feel compelled to agree with everyone, nor do we need people to like us. We're much more resilient to shame. We're not afraid to show our weaknesses, wobbly bits or vulnerabilities. We also take care of ourselves. And life becomes more fluid.

Sometimes this stage creeps up on us. One day we just realize that we've been feeling different for a while. It can even occur overnight, with the sudden realization and solid conviction that we're going to live life in a new way, from a new mindset.

Many people reach this stage in the later years of their life, although that doesn't mean we can't reach it at any time. It's just an observation that I have made that most people take some time to believe they are *enough*. Some reach it through a release; they feel battle-weary. Others just gradually *emerge* into it.

It's a state of contentment. We cease to resist life and in doing so actually have more influence over our life. It's also a state of gratitude, both for the people and for the content of our life.

In many ways, we resemble our child self. Young children don't question their worth. They don't even know what worth is. But their behaviour shows a complete acceptance of themselves, which we adults know as self-love.

When their daughter, Alyx, was about 18 months old, my friends Bryce and Allyson brought her to visit us for a few days. One night after dinner, Bryce asked her, 'Are you brilliant, Alyx?' She responded, '*Yeeeeessssss.*' Then she hugged herself. Next, she stood in front of our full-length mirror and gave her own reflection a kiss.

People who know they are *enough* don't question their worth either. Self-love is an assumption that comes across in their nature. And, just like children, some of them play more.

You can easily spot a person who knows they're *enough*. Usually, they're very likeable. They don't expend any effort convincing you of their good points and achievements but often take an active interest in yours.

In this book, I'm going to offer you some simple tips and strategies that will help you live from a state of *enough*. I'm going to take you to the self-love gym.

The Self-Love Gym

There are lots of exercises spread throughout this book. You don't need to do all of them, but I'd advise you to do the ones that resonate with you and also the ones that stretch you or push you out of your comfort zone a little. I think of this as going to the gym for your soul – a self-love gym.

The key with going to the self-love gym is consistent practice, just as consistent workouts in a physical gym are the key to building physical fitness. There are a few exercises that require you to repeat the same thing, just as you might do 10 reps of a leg curl, for example. Other exercises are more reflective or ask you to make choices or decide on action steps. All of the exercises are designed to help you attain the mental and emotional fitness of 'I *am* enough.' They place your mind and emotions into that state – even if just for a short space of time at first. The effect of this is to wire that state into the networks of your brain. You'll learn more about that later on.

You're Only Human

One of the many things I'll remind you of as you go through this book is that you're only human. No one goes through life without making mistakes. No one goes through life without having a bad day. Most people have lots of them in fact. So, if life is tough for you right now, you're definitely not alone. It's tough for a lot of people. Sometimes, just knowing this can make it a little easier. It can make you feel a little less alone. And you *aren't* alone. You are, after all, a member of the human family.

Part of being human is being entitled to be happy. We don't need to earn the right, just as we don't need to earn sunlight or oxygen. We're also entitled to love and health. And we're entitled to thrive. And when I say 'entitled', I mean that there are no questions about this, no arguments, no debates. It just is!

Remember this as you set out on your self-love project. Also remember that there's no hurry to complete that project. I worked on mine for nine months before I submitted the first draft of this book and I still had a long way to go. So, don't put yourself under pressure. Just remind yourself that it's OK to be exactly where you are right now. That will make it easier to move forward.

Here's a brief summary of what we've learned so far:

The three stages of self-love are: 1) 'I'm *not* enough' … which becomes 2) 'I've *had* enough' … which becomes 3) 'I *am* enough.'

Most of us spend most of our time in the first stage, although we don't notice it. It's less of a conscious awareness and more of an assumption about our own worth that causes us to interpret the world and people's behaviour in a certain way.

Needing people to like and approve of us is characteristic of the first stage. Feeling small, irrelevant or low in self-confidence is also common.

In time, we might find that we've *had* enough. It's not just the circumstances of our life and the way people treat us that are the issue here, but the awareness that these actually have a lot to do with our own feelings of worth. So we start to take control again.

It's not uncommon to feel passion and even anger at this stage. It's a stage of much higher energy than *not enough*.

Waiting at the other side of this stage is 'I *am* enough'. At this stage, gone is the sense that we need to prove ourselves to anyone. We don't need people to like us, although we mostly find that they do anyway, because we like ourselves. So we no longer waste energy seeking approval and reassurance, and success and achievement come more easily to us. Life isn't without its challenges, because challenges are normal in the human experience.

But the attitude with which we meet our challenges is 'I *am* enough.' And this breeds happiness and fulfilment.

Chapter 2

Meet the Parents

*'Research indicates that parenting is
a primary predictor of how prone our
children will be to shame or guilt.'*

BRENE BROWN, *DARING GREATLY*

Have you ever noticed that most adults behave like children?

I once worked in an office which, if I'd closed my eyes, I could have mistaken for a room full of children. There were tantrums, door-slammings, name-callings, just about everything you'd expect in a schoolyard apart from having your lunch money stolen or your underpants pulled up your back in a 'wedgy' (although most grown-ups act out an equivalent). Most of the time it was just a normal environment containing kind hard-working people. But when pressed in the wrong way, some in the office reverted to being children.

I suspect you've lived or worked in the same kind of place. I'd be surprised if you haven't. Few adults grow out of that kind of behaviour. You only need to watch a room full of politicians arguing to know exactly what I'm talking about. On the surface, we appear to be grown-ups. We've learned how we're supposed to behave. But push or prod us in the wrong way and maturity goes right out the window.

Some people try to hide their childish behaviour in an effort to be respectable or professional. But behind closed doors, their husband, wife or children get to see their juvenile tendencies play out in their emotional behaviour.

Our Chemical Blend

The reason for a lot of this is a particular blend of brain chemicals.

The brain gets used to things, just as we do. While we might get used to a job, a husband or wife, or even a certain blend of tea, the brain gets used to a certain blend of chemicals. One of these is cortisol, a stress hormone.

This mostly occurs during the first six or seven years of life. It's the result of our most consistent emotional environment. By the age of about seven, the brain has a pretty good idea of what's 'normal', so it 'sets' that level of cortisol and the overall chemical blend.

We take our setting and our blend with us into adulthood. As we move through our adult years, it flavours how we tend to feel about ourselves, how we interpret the world around us and the behaviour of other people, and how we respond to stressors. It's why most of us behave like children.

The cortisol setting and chemical blend aren't genetic, even though a lot of people assume they must be. It's common to believe that genetics are always in charge. This is made worse by large genome programmes being given billions of dollars in investment so that we can identify the 'gene for cancer' or the 'gene for Alzheimer's'. These projects make headline news, but the scientists working on them know it's not nearly as black and white as that. They know that the environment plays a huge role in how a gene behaves.

Unfortunately, by and large the public doesn't know this. So people get the idea that if something's in their genes they can't do anything about it. That's not true at all. With the exception of a very small number of genetic diseases, how a gene behaves is largely down to its environment.

A gene is a bit like a light bulb with a sensor on it that measures how much natural light is around. As the natural light fades in the evening, the light bulb comes on. It's responding to its environment. Our genes do that too. They've always been doing that. That's how they work.

Don't get me wrong – genetics plays a role too, but when it comes to setting the chemistry and even much of the neural architecture of the brain, it's only a minor role. Our environment is much more important. And as small children, our environment was created, most of the time, by our parents.

Self-Worth Contagion

Let's give the self-worth setting a scale of one to ten. If your mum had a self-worth setting of, say, seven, and your dad four, and you were closer to your mum, you'd probably have a self-worth setting of seven as well, or maybe six, depending on the amount of time you spent with your dad. This is because in your early years, when your brain was growing fast, you would mainly have been in an environment created by your mum. It's what I call 'self-worth contagion'.

It's not always quite so black and white of course, because other people influence us as well – grandparents, for instance, and even schoolteachers. And sometimes just a one-off event, or even a sentence, resonates with us at a deep subconscious level and has a significant effect. So there are always exceptions. There's always the person who grows up in a houseful of twos but emerges as a nine, or grows up in environments of eights but moves through life as a three. But most people, most of the time, will have a self-worth setting pretty close to that of their parents.

If you're a parent and you have low self-esteem, don't worry! Now you understand the self-worth contagion effect, you can help your children have a much healthier level of self-esteem. It starts with simply being aware of it. Then you can put into practice some of what you learn from this book. And as your own self-esteem rises and you meet the world in a whole new way, you'll help your children further, as they'll learn from your words and actions.

Like most parents, my mum and dad didn't know anything about self-worth contagion. Personally, I'd estimate that my mum met the world as a three and my dad as a four. At such low levels, the concept of high self-worth can be hard to grasp, regardless of what you're doing in your life, because there's no frame of reference, no experience of high self-worth, available to you. It's like trying to imagine a colour that doesn't exist.

Meeting the world with low self-worth has become a habit for many people and I'll take a guess that you count yourself in this. Regardless of what's happening around you, what's being said or how people are behaving, your brain is so used to interpreting the world in a particular way that you've never thought to question it. If good things are happening or nice things are being said, your assumption will be that these are one-off events or people are 'just saying that' or it'll blow over you without resonating with you at all. Low self-worth will even cause you to misinterpret people's words and intentions, because your brain is trying hard to maintain the levels of chemicals it considers normal. Many people with low self-worth will go to the ends of the Earth to find the insult behind the compliment.

Quite often people marry a person with a similar level of self-worth to their own. We attract people who will bring us the kind of experiences and validation that our brain chemistry is most used to. It's not at all uncommon for a person with low self-love to shun a mate who will help them to have a happy life in favour of one who will bring them the levels of stress, anxiety and depression that their brain has been conditioned to expect.

But there is hope – of course there is, otherwise I wouldn't have written this book! Self-love can be learned at any age with a little bit of consistent thought and practice. We'll find out how later. But first, here's some more on parental influences, just to give you a richer understanding of how we develop and to help you change even faster.

How We Learn to Question Our Worth

At a conference recently, I heard Michael Neill, author of *Feel Happy Now*, say, 'You were born happy. You weren't born needing therapy.'

It's so true! Happy is how we start out. We have healthy self-worth then, too. Most of us lose it as we grow up and spend the rest of our life trying to find it again, but young children don't question their worth at all. Not at first. They learn to do it through their experiences with adults.

Quite simply, young children take on board whatever adults tell them. If the words and actions of the adults convey to them they are *not* enough, they'll know they're *not* enough. If the words and actions of the adults show them they *are* enough, they'll know that instead.

How does it happen? There are three main ways.

1) Being Shamed

Some parents use shame as a parenting style. It's mostly because they've never learned anything else. They were shamed by their parents, and their parents by theirs before them. Shaming is a style that passes through the generations, just like genes. It's a way of correcting behaviour. But there's a downside to telling a child that they're bad, a liar or a good for nothing. It doesn't come from the reprimand. The problem is in the use of the words 'You are' followed by something bad. That's shaming, and childhood is where it starts.

The point is that there's a world of difference between *telling a lie* and *being a liar*. Telling a lie is a form of behaviour, and behaviour can be changed. But if a child believes they are a liar, that requires a change of identity. That's a much bigger thing to change and the thought of it can leave children feeling hopeless. So they accept their given identity, and some rebel, lie, cheat and steal as an expression of it. Ultimately, shame corrodes self-worth. But later in the book you'll learn how to become resilient to shame.

Most parents don't mean to shame their children. They've no idea that the language has any negative effect at all.

One of the most empowering communications with a child I ever heard was in a movie called *The Help*, based on a book by Kathryn Stockett. I've not read the book, but in the movie, the black nanny repeatedly says to the white child in her care that she is good, she is kind and she is important. The child is then invited to repeat it back to the nanny. This, to me, is a very empowering message to give a child, one that can only strengthen their sense of worth. It gives the child a positive sense of identity through the words, 'You are' followed by something good.

My friend Lizzie, however, pointed out that many parents, her own included, would have been horrified by a child affirming her worth in this way, believing that she was being encouraged to be 'too big for her boots'. I heard that term a lot in the village I grew up in, too, and at the school I attended. Unfortunately, a consequence of not wanting to be 'too big for your boots' can be a lifetime of playing small and apologetic, which gives birth to a sense of *not* enough and also interferes with achievement. I can say this from personal experience.

Another version of the term used in my village and school was 'If she [or he] was chocolate, she would eat herself.' Similarly, the result of this is that to avoid being singled out and rejected by the community, children learn to play small, and thus the seeds of *not enough* are sown.

2) Being Criticized

The second way children learn to doubt their worth is through being criticized. Some are criticized for doing things wrongly or badly. Others are compared to a sibling who does things correctly. Some parents even swear or sneer at their children.

Now and again, a little piece of criticism is OK if it's well intentioned, but for some children it is consistent, and that's how brain networks are shaped. The fact that the parents are trying to educate the child and help them grow doesn't change the point that consistent criticism can give rise to a feeling of *not* enough. A parent says, 'You're doing it wrong,' and what they mean is 'It will be/you will be better if you do it this way.' What the child hears is 'You're not good enough right now.' In time, the child learns at a subconscious level that they are *not* enough.

Many children have critical parents who push them to excel academically. If the child gets a 'B', the reaction is kind enough, but it is often along the lines of, 'Maybe if you work even harder you'll get an "A" next time.' What the child hears is, 'You're not working hard enough right now.' Sometimes, parents even launch into a lecture about how well they did at school or university.

All this can give rise to decades of trying to prove yourself to a parent. Many high-fliers in life are like this, perfectionists needing to be the best, powerfully driven by a sense of lack that, they believe, will one day be filled by achievement. But they completely lack the understanding that lack of worth can never be filled by achievement. Only knowing you *are* enough will fill the void.

3) Through Observation

The third way we learn to doubt our worth is through observing the behaviour of those around us, particularly our primary care-giver. My mum had low self-esteem when I was a child and I was there when she acted out her feelings about herself, so I learned to act the same way – not because she told me this was how I should behave, but simply because it was what I learned from her. In fact, she'd learned to doubt her own worth when *she* was a child.

As an eight-year-old, my mum had watched her mum have a stroke that left her paralysed down one side and unable to speak. My granny collapsed on the stairs and clutched hold of the banister. My Aunty Jane, Mum's elder sister, who was 17 at the time, screamed, 'Go get my daddy!' He worked about a mile away. Mum ran along the road as fast as her legs would carry her and returned with my papa. Granny was taken to hospital.

Granny had always done all the washing and cleaning, and when she was recovering from the stroke, the rest of the family had to take over. My papa was working long hours and my mum's two elder sisters were at the age where they were out a lot with boys. Mum felt that she had to learn to do everything for herself, and also help look after her two younger brothers. One day, a couple of years later, the schoolteacher took her aside and told her that the ribbons in her hair were dirty, and that even though her mum was disabled she was old enough to take better care of herself. While this was well intentioned, telling a young girl who is close to puberty that she is dirty is about the worst thing in the world. Through no fault of her own, Mum developed a deep belief that she was less worthy than everyone else.

She has also had little self-confidence as an adult, which is not surprising. And building my own self-confidence has been one of my biggest challenges in life.

Parents

Some parents have very few parenting skills. In the area where I grew up, most of our neighbours were kind and friendly people. But it wasn't uncommon to hear young children being called all sorts of language that I wouldn't dare replicate in this book. So often I would hear a parent angrily saying, 'Dare you look at me!' or 'I'll make you laugh on the other side of your face.' These words always seemed to be communicated in rage. It would be little wonder if those children grew up to have low self-esteem.

I grew up in a typical working-class environment. My parents never pushed me towards higher education because no one in our family had ever gone to college or university. It always seemed above us. It was my chemistry teacher, Mr Tracey, who first planted the seed in my mind when I was 16 years old, shortly after I'd received exam results that included an 'A' for chemistry.

When he first mentioned it, my immediate reaction was shock. I couldn't possibly go to university. I wasn't intelligent enough and my family didn't have enough money. These things I knew.

I also knew, as naïve as it might sound, that there were only two universities in the UK – Oxford and Cambridge. I knew that from watching the annual boat race on TV. You needed to be rich to get into places like that, and posh. Only people like Michael Thom and Paul Tortolano, two very intelligent middle-class boys in my class, could possibly go to university. And maybe Big Vince Kolosowski as well. Even though he was from a similar background to me, he was way cleverer than everyone else.

University wasn't the norm in our village. But I had a very positive influence in my mum. Several times when I was growing up, she would say, 'Stick in at school so you can do well and get a better life than the one your daddy and I have had.' I heard it so many times. I still hear it today in my head like a mantra.

So I went to university to study chemistry. The lack of parental pressure on me meant that university was all about learning things that fascinated me. I loved chemistry. I loved learning the structure of molecules and how to build them. I also loved doing calculations in some of my classes where chemistry, physics and mathematics overlapped. I really loved learning.

I knew one or two girls and boys in some of my classes who were very driven. They were always in the top few per cent academically. They were also the most stressed. The two seemed to go hand in hand. They were rarely satisfied with their performances in exams. Looking back, I'd say they also suffered from depression, although they hid it well.

Many of the students from working-class backgrounds similar to my own were more laid-back and had a much easier time at university.

This observation is reflected in a study led by psychologists who compared academically strong middle-class girls with working-class girls all the way from the ages of four to 19.[1] By the time they were 19, the middle-class girls were much more stressed and anxious than the working-class ones. The cause seemed to be that they didn't feel that their achievements were good enough.

Most of the time, girls who fall into this category have pushy parents or parents whose coaching style is critical. The trouble with criticism as a parenting or coaching style is that it teaches you that you're *not* enough now. You'll only be enough when you achieve such and such a thing.

Critical parents don't mean to communicate this, of course. Mostly they're just trying to get their children to realize their potential. But if the children do become high-achieving adults and the parents believe they were right to push them, research indicates that the high achievers are statistically more likely to have low self-esteem than average achievers. Having pushy parents is a breeding ground for depression.

In a study of American girls from affluent backgrounds, more than 20 per cent suffered from serious depression.[2] That figure is only 7 per cent in the general population,[3] so you can immediately see the effects of being pushed, or coached with criticism.

Some children who are pushed to succeed learn to attach their self-worth to the achievement of goals because achieving was their only way of being validated by a parent who usually pushed or criticized them. As adults, if they succeed, they feel good. If they fail, unless they have learned self-compassion, their self-worth takes a beating.

By the time they become adults, many of these people have learned to set completely unrealistic targets. Deep down, they eventually expect to fail, and that will return them to the level of self-worth that they're used to feeling, retaining the brain chemistry that their brain knows best. Yet at the same time, they strive to succeed in the belief that success will bring them self-worth.

This isn't meant to be a class comparison, just a way of pointing out that many middle-class and upper-class parents push their children to succeed because they've learned the value of success in their own life and they want their children to succeed and be comfortable. This often works in the success stakes, but can have negative consequences in the mental health and self-esteem stakes, especially if the parental coaching strategy has predominantly used criticism. Children need guidance and boundaries, but they also need to learn that they are *good enough* just as they are, and they need to be able to make their own choices and learn the likely consequences of those choices.

In essence, we learn how we should be treated by how our parents treat us. As children, we are far more observant than our parents think. We learn how we should be spoken to by the way they speak to us. We learn how we should behave by watching how they behave and we learn how we should interact with people by watching how they interact with people. We even notice whether we are treated more or less fairly than anyone else – a sibling, for instance. Seeing a sibling getting preferential treatment can bring on a self-love deficit early on. We deduce that they are better than we are. By inference, 'I am *not* enough.'

Of course, children are not always quite so sensitive. Most children are highly resilient and are unlikely to be affected by the odd throwaway comment or situation where another child appears to be favoured over them. It's mostly behaviour or treatment that is consistent over a period of time that affects how a child feels about themself and their place in the world.

It's Not about Blame

Before we go any further, I want to make it clear that this isn't about blaming our parents for any challenges we have with our self-esteem. The vast majority of parents want the best for their children and do what they believe is best for their children.

While I don't have any human children as I write this, I am 'daddy' to Oscar. He can be a nervous dog at times. His big YouTube hit[4] sees him afraid to cross the threshold of our front door to begin his first walk as a three-month-old puppy. He's still very much the same today – not with leaving our house, but with going into other people's houses.

As well as self-love, some of my major life challenges have been its offspring – self-confidence, fear and anxiety. It is possible, likely even, that Oscar somehow learned some habits from me. With hindsight, I probably would have done some things differently when he was a puppy. At the time, though, I thought I was doing what was best for Oscar.

While he is unlikely to blame me for his challenges (mostly because he's a dog), I would hope that if he were human, he would understand that I, too, have had my difficulties in life but have always loved him very much and always acted in the way I felt was best at the time. If he himself ever became a parent, I'd hope he'd pass the same sentiment on to his puppies.

Understanding, rather than blame, has to be the way forward for all of us.

Let's start by taking a trip to the self-love gym...

- -

SELF-LOVE GYM:
How Much Are You Like Your Parents?

♦ If you're really honest, how much do you resemble either your mum or dad, or both your parents, in:

　...your behaviour?

　...your attitude and thinking?

　...your beliefs?

　...how you react to challenges?

　...how you look at people or the world?

◆ Are there any themes in your life that are similar to those of either or both of your parents? For instance, are you with a similar partner to your mum or dad, or does your theme of success or failure follow that of either of your parents, or do you have similar health conditions? Similar themes indicate similar beliefs, mindsets, ways of looking at the world and self-worth.

◆ If you have identified similarities to your parents that are not serving you, think about how you could change your thoughts, actions and beliefs to declare that you are enough. Then write them down. For instance, you might write:

> *'Even though my parents had low self-worth, I am now moving through life with confidence, courage and respect for myself.'*

Or, if you have the same lifestyle-related health issue as a parent, you might write:

> *'I am the master of my health. I am inspired to eat nutritious food and I treat my body with love and respect.'*

Or perhaps you've identified a similarity with financial struggle, in which case you might write something like:

> *'I no longer repeat the financial fortunes of my parents. Every day I am making inspired choices and putting ideas into practice that are reaping great financial rewards.'*

◆ Repeat these statements 10 times each morning and 10 times each evening.

It's empowering to recognize that life is not happening to you, but that learned patterns are shaping many of its events and circumstances. The power in this exercise is in recognizing the patterns in your life that you have learned from your parents and prising yourself away from those that don't serve you anymore.

Some of us have had good childhoods, others more difficult ones. Complete the following exercise if you feel that your low self-worth was shaped by your childhood.

SELF-LOVE GYM:
How Did Your Self-Worth Issues Arise?

♦   Did your parents often praise you? Did they criticize you? Did they shame you?

♦   How did your mum typically speak to you? What about your dad? Your siblings?

♦   Did any of your school experiences affect your sense of self-worth? If so, which?

♦   Did anyone else, or any other situation, mould your self-worth?

♦   Estimate the self-worth levels of your parents.

♦   If you were to estimate your own level of self-worth, how closely would it match that of your parents?

Trying to Do What's Best

As I mentioned earlier, it's quite important that you don't go blaming your parents for your self-worth difficulties. If your life hasn't gone to plan so far, it's easy to conclude that it was the fault of your mother or father, but most parents are simply trying to do the best they can do given their knowledge and experiences in life. Many are also trying to balance their responsibilities as parents with the other pressures, often financial and work-related.

If you do find yourself angry about your childhood, try the following exercise to understand your parents better.

Please note that this exercise isn't intended for people who have been abused or badly mistreated. If you have suffered severe abuse, I'd recommend you speak to a trained and compassionate specialist.

. . . .

♥️ SELF-LOVE GYM: *What Was Their Intention?*

Thinking about how your parents behaved towards you as a child, ask yourself, 'What was their intention?'

Sit with the question for a little while. Try putting yourself in their shoes. Do you really think they intended to make you unhappy? Could it be that they were just trying to do what they thought was best for you? Perhaps they wanted you to be successful in the world and were so passionate about your potential that they pressured you because they wanted you to realize it, believing it would make you happiest in the long term.

. . . .

Parents often want more for their children than they had themselves. But they may not fully explain that to their children and it's easy to misinterpret their actions as not loving their children.

A lot of parents are just trying to do what they believe is best given their knowledge, experience and resources, and these won't be infallible. Parents screw up. People screw up. Everybody screws up. But everybody is trying to do the best they can. Welcome to life!

If we can accept that no one's perfect, we can start to untangle some of our emotions. We can even learn to laugh at what happened to us in the past. We can laugh at ourselves, not in a berating, judgemental way but in a compassionate way that says, 'This is what I did or how I was – how insane was that?! Ha, ha, ha!'

Our Responsibility as Parents

If you are a parent yourself, through understanding the roots of your own sense of self-worth you can effectively empower your own children. And empower them you can. Whether you are a parent or a teacher, an educator, carer, aunt, uncle, family friend or neighbour, you can have an impact on the self-esteem of children.

It's up to us all, as parents, educators or family, to teach children in ways that give them self-worth.

If we criticize them, they learn to criticize themselves and others.

If we teach them acceptance and understanding, they learn to accept themselves and others.

If we show them how to be grateful, they learn to appreciate themselves and others.

But if we teach them shame, they learn to hold back and be apprehensive.

If we show them honesty, they learn to be honest with themselves and fair with others.

If we share with them, they learn to be kind.

If we teach them friendliness, they learn to bond and form relationships.

And if we teach them that they *are* enough, they learn that they *are* enough and their future is bright!

> **In summary... We learn to have low self-esteem. It's often through being shamed, being criticized or being in the presence of a person (or people) with low self-esteem and learning from their habits.**
>
> **Of course, most parents don't intend to sap self-worth from their children. They usually learned their parenting strategies from their own parents, who learned from theirs, and so on. Most parents simply want what's best for their children and we can help ourselves to move on in life if we remember that.**
>
> **Is there any advantage to understanding that a self-love deficit was learned? Yes, there's a huge advantage. The first step towards a healthy level of self-esteem is *realizing* that it was learned. We then naturally arrive at**

the conclusion that we weren't born that way. If we feel unworthy of love, happiness, money, great relationships, success or anything else that life has to offer, it's simply down to what we've learned. And this insight is where the magic lies, because if we've learned it, we can also unlearn it.

Read on and find out how...

Chapter 3

How to Use Your Body to Change How You Feel

'Our bodies change our minds.'
AMY CUDDY

When I was child at school, I remember being taught a little song that I later learned was from *The King and I*. It was about making believe you were brave even when you were afraid. Fake it 'til you make it!

When we feel happy, it's usually written all over our face. It also comes across in our body language: our shoulders, the way we walk, stand or sit, how we breathe. The same can be said when we're feeling sad or stressed: our face and body convey it.

This much most people know, but what few know is that it goes the other way too. Just as our mind affects our body, our body also affects our mind.

A lot of what we now know about this comes from studying animals. If a dog is nervous, notice that its tail tucks into its rear. If you lift its tail up, it actually lifts the dog's confidence.

We can consciously use our body to change how we feel about ourselves. In my experience, it's actually about the fastest way to change how you feel at any moment.

It works because body and mind are intertwined. Most people think of emotion as just a feeling, but did you know that it is actually smeared throughout your body?

The Four Components of Emotion

The diagram below shows what I call our 4-Component Emotion (4CE).

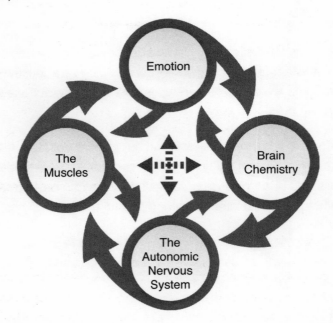

1) Emotion

The first component is, well, emotion.

2) Brain Chemistry

An emotion is connected to the brain chemistry of that emotion. That basically means that when we feel happy, our brain produces serotonin, dopamine and sometimes endogenous opiates, the brain's own versions of morphine and heroin. These are all happy chemicals. When we feel happy, we produce happy chemistry.

3) The Autonomic Nervous System

Our autonomic nervous system (ANS) also shows the emotion. This basically means our skin and organs respond to the emotion. It's why our palms sweat when we feel anxious and it's why our heart races when we see someone we love.

I sometimes use a heart monitor when I teach. It swiftly and clearly shows how the rhythm of the heart responds to what a person is thinking or feeling.

The fact that the ANS is linked with emotion also explains why mental and emotional stress is linked with cardiovascular disease and even why being consistently hostile and aggressive is one of the fastest ways to harden up our arteries.

4) The Muscles

Emotion is also connected to our muscles. We don't smile when we're happy, for example, because we think we're supposed to; we smile because it's a reflex reaction due to the fact that our emotions are entangled with our facial muscles.

It's Multi-Directional

All the arrows go all ways, too – it's 'multi-directional'. Just as emotion affects facial muscles and body language, so facial muscles and body language also affect emotion.

Not only does emotion affect heart rhythm, for example, but changes in heart rhythm affect how we feel. A racing heart might make us feel anxious while a calm heart might make us feel peaceful. This is the strategy behind beta-blockers (which steady the heart rhythm). Training our autonomic nervous system can therefore increase positive emotion.

Changes in brain chemistry also affect emotion (as well as vice versa). In fact, the entire pharmaceutical model for depression uses this single observation. If you get an increase in serotonin levels by taking an antidepressant drug, for instance, it will make you feel happier. You can also give a person a high with a drug that alters brain chemistry.

Despite this being the most common approach to treating depression, however, it is only one part of a more holistic approach. There are many different groups of thought on how to alleviate depression. Some people swear that drugs are the only way; others say nutrition is better. Actually, both affect our brain chemistry and this then affects our emotions. Some say a regular meditation practice is the best, others say it's all about releasing suppressed emotion and yet others insist it's all about finding meaning and purpose in life. All three of these approaches relax the ANS, though, and this then has a net positive effect on emotion. They are really just different parts of the same phenomenon: *emotion is literally smeared throughout the body*.

So we can change how we feel by i) using our mind; ii) improving our nutrition or taking medicines that impact brain chemistry; iii) calming our nervous system; or iv) moving our body in a way that reflects how we want to feel. They all work. But the fastest of these at changing how we feel at any given moment, and the easiest way to produce long-term changes, is using our body.

If we want to feel stressed, for example, we can get there pretty quickly if we start moving our body in a jerky fashion and speaking more quickly. We can speed it up even more if we take shallow breaths.

This is great news! Why? It shows that moving our body can produce the feelings we want to produce.

So, if we want to feel happy, we can move our body in a way that says, 'I feel happy!' And lo and behold, we will feel happy.

Surely it can't be that simple? Surely everyone would be doing it if it were?

The trouble is, hardly anyone knows anything about this. It's hardly a mainstream idea yet. Unless you happen to study neuroscience or read one of the popular science and self-help books out there, chances are you won't have heard of it. It always amazes me to see eyes widen in surprise each time I present this kind of stuff to professional audiences. It's almost always completely new information.

Some clever therapists are, however, already suggesting that some of their clients or patients do in fact fake it 'til they make it. 'Laugh doctor' Cliff Kuhn is one of them. He encourages patients with depression to laugh and smile on purpose. He reports that, 'Those willing to practise it experience mood elevation and a reduction in symptoms – almost instantaneously.'[1]

And it's based on real research. Simply using facial muscles, researchers at the University of Alaska, Anchorage, asked volunteers to look at photographs of people who were either smiling or frowning. Half of the volunteers were asked simply to look at the faces but the other half were asked to copy either the smile or the frown. Immediately afterwards they had their mood assessed. Those who copied a smile enjoyed a more positive mood. Those who copied a frown felt less positive. Those who simply looked at the faces didn't feel any different. Interestingly, the results were even more pronounced when the volunteers copied the facial expressions while looking at themselves in a mirror.[2]

In these instances it was the movement of the muscles of the face in a way that the brain recognized was correlated with happiness that produced the more positive feelings. Moving other areas of our body works in the same way. Swinging our arms joyfully as we walk will elevate our mood, while slouching and staring at the ground will depress it.

If you've tried unsuccessfully to improve your happiness or self-love in the past, the problem could be that you didn't get your body in synch with what you were trying to do with your mind. The moment you start using your body to create happiness you'll probably notice that you've really not been making happy movements with your body at all. In fact, you'll probably notice that a great many of the movements you do make – how you stand and hold your body most of the time, how you speak – actually convey unhappiness or low self-worth.

Initially, as you start to pay more attention to your body, you might notice that your facial muscles or your jaw are quite often tight, or perhaps your shoulders are raised a lot of the time. You might also catch yourself taking shallow breaths. All of these body conditions show stress, unhappiness or low self-worth and therefore contribute to feelings of stress, unhappiness or low self-worth.

It produces a yo-yo effect: you make an improvement through doing some mental practices but then you snap back into feeling the way you've always felt.

Fake It and You'll Make It: The Harvard Power Pose

In *The Expression of Emotion in Man and Animals*, Charles Darwin wrote, 'Even the simulation of an emotion tends to arouse it in our minds.'

Smiling is the essence of one component of laughter yoga. Try it now. Take a deep breath, pull your face into a large smile, then exhale and let out a little chuckle. It reduces blood pressure (ANS) and it produces serotonin, dopamine and endorphins (happy chemistry) in the brain. It also makes you feel better. Basically, a happy face produces happy chemistry.

Using facial muscles to affect emotion is known as the facial feedback hypothesis. It was first put forward by William James over 100 years ago. According to this hypothesis, facial muscles actually feed back into the brain and bring about the emotional state associated with those muscle movements.

In the 1990s, psychologist Paul Eckman showed that smiling or grimacing produced changes throughout the ANS. When he asked volunteers to smile or grimace, he recorded changes in their heart rate and skin conductance. When they smiled, heart rate and skin conductance decreased.[3]

This is all very important in relation to self-love. When you feel you're *not* enough, the feeling is smeared throughout your body. It's in your brain chemistry, your autonomic nervous system and your muscles. So what if you pretended to be *enough*? What if you wore *enough* all over your body?

It can actually change how you feel about yourself very quickly. In little experiments I've conducted in some of my workshops, people notice a real difference in just a few minutes.

Participants are asked to adopt the body language of *not* enough. Most lean their head forwards and look down at the floor, adopting a serious or sad expression. Some shuffle their feet or take small steps that are overly mechanical as if they are having to concentrate on how to walk. They almost always tense their upper body. After doing this for two minutes, most report that they feel less positive than they did before they started. One man joked he felt 'downright miserable'.

Then they quickly swap their body language to say 'I *am* enough.' You can see immediate and significant changes in posture. Some people look as though they've grown five inches as they stand up straight, lengthening their spine. Movements are more fluid, slow and relaxed. Faces tend to show relaxed, serene and happy expressions. Heads sit comfortably on shoulders and eyes tend to face front.

Despite all these obvious changes, the transition in their emotional state is what participants notice most. Most people feel much more positive and relaxed in less than 20 seconds. Many report feeling confident and self-assured. Some have an almost overwhelming realization: first that *not* enough is actually how they tend to present themselves and second that they have a tool that can change that really fast.

Exciting new research is adding weight to the understanding of why this works. Drawing comparisons between how humans and primates behave, Harvard professor Amy Cuddy noted that when humans or primates feel powerful, they make their body appear bigger. A primate will raise its arms above its head, for instance. In effect, they become bigger and take up more space.

When people feel nervous before, say, giving a presentation or being interviewed for a job, have you noticed how many shrink in their chairs, curving their spines, or fold their arms, pulling their shoulders forwards and inwards? Nowadays, they also slouch over their phones. In effect, they become smaller.

Cuddy reasoned that if people actually made themselves bigger by adopting a confident, 'high-power' posture, it would affect how they felt. She wrote:

> *'In both human and non-human primates, expansive, open postures reflect high power, whereas contractive, closed postures reflect low power. Not only do these postures reflect power, they also produce it. [My emphasis.]'⁴*

The key is in the last line. I'll repeat it:

> *'Not only do these postures reflect power, they also produce it.'*

Professor Cuddy invited participants to hold a 'power pose' for just two minutes and measured levels of cortisol and testosterone in their saliva before and afterwards.

After only two minutes, the saliva samples showed that those who did the power pose had a 25 per cent reduction in cortisol (i.e. less stress) and an 20 per cent increase in testosterone (i.e. more confidence). In people who did weak poses, i.e. poses which made the body seem smaller and weaker, their chemistry went in the opposite direction: they had 15 per cent increases in cortisol (i.e. more stress) and 10 per cent decreases in testosterone (i.e. less confidence).[5]

The net effect was:

> *Power pose produces confidence.*
> *Weak pose produces fear.*

The experiment showed that the positioning of the body directly affected its chemistry.

It also affected how the participants felt, and you can now understand why – because body posture and chemistry affect emotion. Participants who did the power poses also said they felt powerful and 'in charge'. When Cuddy and her colleagues invited them to participate in a risk-taking game, they were found to be more confident and less afraid to take risks than the people who did the weak poses.

The participants were each given $2 and invited to roll a dice with 50/50 odds of doubling their money or losing it. Eighty-six per cent of the high-power posers took the risk while only 60 per cent of the low-power posers did.[6] Not only did a two-minute power pose increase the chemistry of confidence, but it translated into more confident behaviour too. And remember, this was simply from being conscious of body language for just two minutes!

If you want to know how to do a power pose, think (or look up) Wonder Woman: upright stance, spine erect, head and eyes forwards, legs shoulder-width apart, shoulders back and hands on hips. It also says, 'I *am* enough!'

How We Function is Affected by How We Hold Our Body. Fact!

Cuddy went further with the research and in a separate experiment measured how power poses affected volunteers who were about to give a presentation, something which tends to make most people feel nervous.[7] Could a two-minute power pose affect how a person functioned in the real world?

Half of the volunteers did a two-minute power pose before giving a short presentation, while the other half did a weak pose – the kind most people actually do before a presentation, which betrays the fact that they're nervous or lacking in confidence. A weak pose is one that makes the body smaller in any way: arms folded, shoulders rounded, body leaning forwards, etc.

Their presentations were assessed by a panel, who also rated fluidity of speaking, vocal tone, hesitation, pauses, mistakes, etc. The panel didn't know which pose each person had done, but they rated the presentations given by the power posers as of much higher quality than the presentations of the weak posers. The power posers were more fluid in their communication and showed less reliance on their notes. The weak posers conveyed much less confidence; they stuttered more and used their notes more.

The judges were also asked whom they would employ if the presentation had been part of a job interview. Their choices were always those who had power-posed.

In some of my talks and workshops on self-love, I enjoy getting the entire audience power posing for two minutes. I time it. It's surprising how long two minutes feels when you're standing in a silent room full of people in a power pose. It's actually a lot of fun and produces quite a bit of laughter.

Think of how your own daily interactions might be different if you practised power posing!

A few weeks after I taught power posing during a talk I delivered at a conference, I received an e-mail which said:

'I was due to go for a first interview a few days after the love course and I just wanted to drop you a line and say thank you for the power pose … I felt a bit of a prat standing next to my car in the Coventry Arena doing it. So much so that I opted to visualize doing it in my head for the second interview, but it still had the same effect. And I got the job.'

New research studies are adding weight to that fact that body posture affects how we feel. In a 2014 study by scientists at the University of Auckland, New Zealand, 74 participants were asked to sit in an upright or slumped position. They even had their backs strapped with physiotherapy tape to ensure their posture remained constant. Then they were given a stressful task whereby they had to tell a panel why they were the best candidate for a fictitious dream job, having only about five minutes to prepare. Those who sat in an upright position reported higher self-esteem than those who sat slumped. They also had more positive moods and lower fear. The scientists even noted that they used more positive words than those who sat slumped. They were also more effective.[8]

Stand as Though You're Enough and Wire Your Brain Networks

Our muscles, posture, body language, breathing, heart rate and many other physiological parameters not only affect our physical chemistry but also affect our brain networks. Furthermore, consistent changes in any of these also change our brain networks. For example, people who meditate regularly tend to have more connections in the front part of their brain above the eyes, an area known as the prefrontal cortex. It thickens and becomes denser in connections *on account of* the meditation practice.

Most of us never change how we hold our body unless we've had an injury and have been taught by a physical therapist, osteopath or chiropractor to stand or walk in a new way. So our brain networks don't change that much. But if we were to stand or walk differently – say, moving from *not* enough to *enough* – then our brain networks would change to reflect this.

Why is changing brain networks important? Because when the wiring in the brain changes, we don't have to think about something anymore. It becomes automatic. In this case, *enough* becomes our natural state.

This all happens because the brain is highly *neuroplastic*. This means it changes all the time in accordance with how we move, what we learn and even how we think. Remember the thicker prefrontal cortices that were caused by meditation practice? Practice is the key. The brain doesn't change on its own – *it's the things we do that change our brain.*

So, as we learn to stand, walk and behave in a way that says 'I *am* enough', the circuit wiring in our brain will start to change. Before long, the wiring of 'I *am* enough' will take root and what started out as a practice of remembering to hold and move our body in a certain way will become a habit. It will become effortless, because our brain has changed. And as we keep up our effortless new habit, the wiring of 'I'm *not* enough' will begin to disconnect and dissipate.

Simply through holding our body in a certain way, we can actually wire a neurological state and emotional feeling into our brain and body.

. . . .

SELF-LOVE GYM: *Your 'I Am Enough' Pose*

OK, so I want you to practise this. Brain changes occur on account of consistent practice, not through trying something out once, thinking, *Oh good, I know how to do that now*, and then doing nothing more about it (which is what a lot of people do).

♦ Play around with your posture, breathing and facial expressions until you get a sense of what would say 'I *am* enough' for you. It might simply be the Wonder Woman pose. Or it might just be a relaxed posture with an erect spine, loose shoulders and hands by your sides. Find the posture that's right for you.

♦ Also, play around with the way you speak. Let 'I *am* enough' be reflected in your vocal tone and the rate and control of your speech.

♦ Test it out walking, too. A good way to do this is to take an empowering affirmation and literally wear it! For example, the first time I did this was after a situation with an aggressive person. The affirmation I created was '*Today I love myself more than I've ever done before. I have only positive interactions with people and I carry myself with confidence and pride.*' I wore that affirmation all over my body as I walked. I let it diffuse through my face, my shoulders and my breath. The effect was huge and it happened very quickly! An affirmation does become much stronger when your posture helps wire its meaning into your brain.

Once you've got your body posture sorted, here's what to do next:

◆ Pay attention to your body language over the next few days and practise changing how you feel by changing your body: how you walk, stand, sit, breathe; what you do with your head, shoulders, chest, etc. The more you try it, the easier it'll become and the faster it'll work.

◆ Practise your 'I *am* enough' pose as often as you can.

◆ Choose a specific situation where you typically show low self-worth. For example, do you feel self-conscious in some social or professional situations? Do you act submissively around certain people, effectively giving your personal power away? Whatever the situation, do your 'I *am* enough' pose before you enter it and then enter it walking and talking in 'I *am* enough' mode. Notice how you feel. Make a note of any differences from the usual outcome.

◆ Any time you feel you're not enough, shift into your 'I *am* enough' pose. The more you practise it, the better you'll get at it. This is because each time you're wiring 'I *am* enough' more deeply into your brain networks.

Love Thy Selfie

Taking 'selfies' – a photo of yourself taken by yourself while holding a camera – is a bit of a craze these days. I've taken quite a few myself. It's fun. Each time I put on a big smile. It always looks as though I'm having a great time. When we take selfies we all go into 'autopose', an automatic smile or gesture that gives the impression that we're having the time of our life. But are we?

As you know, I'm a firm believer in 'fake it 'til you make it', but the faking has to be done with *intent*. It has to be a full-on *conscious* pretend, performed with the awareness that pretending with intent can actually bring about the feelings you want.

But it's also OK to have a bad day and not feel under pressure to do your 'I *am* enough' pose. It's OK to feel a little sad. Sometimes it's needed and can lead you to an insight about something that's causing some pain in your life. Sometimes, it can lead you to nurturing yourself. It's perfectly OK just to be yourself, however you're feeling. It's a big part of what self-love is. If that means happy, so be it. If it means sad, so be it.

Love your selfie regardless!

In summary... Most of us understand that our emotions affect our body; when we feel emotionally tense, our body will also tense. When we feel happy, our face relaxes, we smile and our breathing is more fluid.

But it goes in reverse too. Tensing our body can make us feel emotionally tense, while relaxing our face, smiling and breathing fluidly can actually make us feel happier. Research at Harvard University has shown that just two minutes of intentional body posture can affect body chemistry and feelings of confidence.

So, if feelings of low self-worth are reflected in your body, perhaps through stooping, looking down or tensing your shoulders, you can cultivate healthier feelings of self-worth simply by adopting a posture and movements that reflect power. It works really quickly too.

Chapter 4

Visualization

*'See things as you would have them
be instead of how they are.'*
ROBERT COLLIER

When Oscar was seven months old, he jumped up on a man on the street outside our house and dirtied his light grey suit.

The ground was damp, Oscar had been trying to dig a weed out of the garden and I'd taken my eye off him for a few seconds. He's a Labrador and if you know dogs at all, you'll know that a Labrador is everyone's best friend. Or at least that's what *they* think. So Oscar said 'hello' in his usual fashion: paws on the man's midriff, eyes playful, mouth wide open and tongue hanging out.

The man didn't take it well. He shouted angrily at me.

As it was still the early days of my self-love project, I didn't deal with the situation very well at all. At that moment I was no longer an adult (I was 42 at the time), I was a six-year-old child being scolded by my schoolteacher.

Wouldn't life be amazing if we could have another go when we don't perform at our best? How amazing if I could have said to the man, 'Thanks for that! I don't suppose we could do it again? I don't think I stood up for myself very well there, so if you could just step back a wee bit, I'll get Oscar to jump up on you again and then if you give me a dressing-down like you did before, I'll see if I can act like a man this time. Thanks so much.'

Then he says 'yes', we have another go, I perform a wee bit better, ask him if it's OK if we do it again, he says 'yes' and we're off again… We end up doing it 10 times for good measure, then we shake hands, Oscar jumps up at the man to see him off, he and I flash slightly coy smiles at each other and we go on our way, Oscar and I to the park and the man to the dry-cleaner.

Wouldn't it be great if life were like this? In some ways, it can be. At least it can be *inside our mind*. And the cool thing about that is, our brain can't tell whether it's really happening or whether we're imagining it.

No, really, our brain doesn't distinguish real from imaginary. We can replay a situation over and over in a new way in our mind and it will become real for our brain, *at least for the wiring of our brain*. And that's the key thing.

So, if we imagine behaving as *enough*, our brain networks will change to reflect 'I *am* enough.'

The Three Rules of Mental Practice

There are three important things to remember about using this technique: *Repetition! Repetition! Repetition!*

OK, so there's really just one thing to remember: you have to do it over and over again.

It's really much the same as going to the gym to get fit, to have a cardio workout or to build muscle. No one ever became Olympic champion after going to the gym just the once!

I've noticed that when people engage in self-help work, they're looking for the magic bullet, the one insight that will effortlessly change their life forever. But here's the thing: that insight is that *change takes repetition*. Change comes when we put insight into practice and do it *consistently*! That's what most people miss. It's the consistency that wires neural networks.

Basically, consistent practice – physically or in our imagination – can wire networks of 'I *am* enough.' And once the networks have built up, our *enough* thinking and behaviour will become automatic. Our brain isn't hardwired. It's in a constant state of flux, responding moment by moment to our thoughts and movements and what we learn and experience in life.

Neuroplasticity

Most people, professionals and some academics included, assume that the brain *is* hardwired. This popular attitude is why we get the idea that change is so difficult.

As a university student in the late eighties and early nineties, I learned that in childhood the brain was like dough. Easy to mould. Impressionable. But then sometime in our late teens, the dough went in the oven and came out with a crust on it. Everything was now set. For life. You couldn't change it. The way you were was just the way you were.

This hardwired notion was actually abandoned nearly 20 years ago, although many still believe it. And that belief does make change quite difficult to effect. But the actual truth is that our brain is changing continually and will continue to change until we take our last breath, even if we live until we're over 100. It's called *neuroplasticity*, or brain plasticity.

Copious amounts of research have shown that a person can imagine doing pretty much anything and their brain will react almost as if they were actually doing it. A 2014 search of the PubMed scientific database under 'mental practice' revealed over 30,000 publications.[1] You could imagine swinging a golf club, serving at tennis, playing piano, typing, diving off a springboard, shooting baskets, lifting weights, kicking a ball or even moving an impaired limb if you had suffered a stroke, and your brain would process it as if you were actually doing it.

In my book *How Your Mind Can Heal Your Body*, I shared research in which the brains of people playing a sequence of piano notes were compared with the brains of people imagining playing the notes. After five days of daily practice, the brains had undergone identical levels of change, with the area connected to the finger muscles growing through neuroplasticity by around 30–40 times. Looking at the brain scans side by side, you couldn't tell who had played the notes from who had imagined playing them.[2]

That wasn't a one-off set of results. neuroplasticity studies that compare imagined practice, the results are the sam. regardless of whether a person is doing som doing it. As already noted, the brain doesn't dis. real and imaginary.

Equally important, however, is that you need to keep doing the work to retain the brain changes. Studies show that if you stop a particular practice or imagined practice, the regions of the brain that have grown simply shrink back down again, just as muscles atrophy when you stop using them. Neuroscientists refer to the phenomenon as 'use it or lose it'.

Have you ever forgotten how to do something? Say long division, for example, that you learned at school? You forgot how to do it because you didn't keep up the practice. The brain networks you built up as you learned it at school simply shrank back down, or disconnected.

Through exactly the same process, you can actually *forget* how to have low self-worth. It may sound impossible to you right now, but as far as your brain is concerned, you simply need to stop practising low self-worth and instead focus on consistently applying the principles and exercises in this book. As you do this, the old wiring will simply dissolve and any feelings of low self-worth will lose their grip on you. You will, essentially, forget how to have low self-love.

Wondering whether it could actually be this simple? Why not give it a try and see for yourself?

...come a Self-Love Olympian

Imagination can be so powerful. Top athletes have learned to appreciate how 'mental practice' can boost their performance. I used to be an athletics coach and the team manager of one of the UK's largest athletic clubs. Once you're in that arena, you swiftly learn just how much mental practice élite athletes do.

I did a corporate talk recently and I spoke after Sally Gunnell, who won the Olympic gold medal in the 400-metre hurdles at the 1992 Barcelona Olympics. She explained that about 70 per cent of winning gold was mental. After failing to win the world championship gold in 1991, she'd hired a sports psychologist. Soon she was visualizing every day. She did loooots of visualization. She practised running and hurdling in her mind.

Importantly, she did a lot of practice on how she'd respond when something went against the plan – when someone overtook her, for instance, or when she had the thought that she wasn't going to win, or when she felt tired. These are the kinds of things that many people forget to do with visualization, but they are just as important as seeing yourself being the best you can be.

Using visualization to improve life performance is exactly the same as using visualization to improve sports performance. You can use it to become an Olympic self-worth champion. I had to use it myself some years ago in a difficult situation.

'You Can F**k Your Decimals!'

This was actually the first thing that was said to me when I started the first class in my new job as maths lecturer.

While writing my first book I accepted two chemistry teaching jobs. One was at the University of Glasgow, where I taught in the Department of Adult and Continuing Education, and the other was at James Watt College of Further & Higher Education. After a few months in the latter, I was asked to teach a basic maths class at a training centre outside the college. It was part of an engineering apprenticeship programme, a regional initiative to provide education and skills to young boys, some of whom came from troubled backgrounds.

I arrived at the centre and entered the class. The noise was deafening. The room was filled with 16-year-old boys, some of whom had been expelled from school, some of whom were in regular trouble with the police, and most of whom had no desire whatsoever to learn maths.

I tried to introduce myself, but I was barely heard above the din. I clapped my hands a few times to get attention. One or two boys looked at me, offering me a glimmer of hope. I couldn't think of anything else to do except start the class. So I did. My first words were: 'We're going to cover decimals this afternoon.' That's when I obtained the advice about what I could do with my decimals, calmly offered by a menacing boy at the front.

They say you can smell fear!

The next hour or so was a disaster. I stuttered and stammered, apologized when someone didn't understand me, and got through about 5 per cent of what I'd intended.

I wanted to run out of the class. In the end, I kind of did. I ended the class 45 minutes early and told the boys that as they'd done so well in their very first class, I was giving them extra time off.

I got into my car, drove out of the town, found the nearest quiet place, pulled over and burst into tears.

I was terrified at the thought of going back into the class the following week. The next day, I went straight to find Fiona, the department head, to tell her I wasn't teaching that class again. If she had a problem with it then I'd be resigning my post as a lecturer.

Fiona wasn't in that day. So I explained what had happened to a colleague, Ian Anton. He burst out laughing. 'We've all had that class,' he explained.

I was adamant *he* hadn't.

He told me that just about every schoolteacher in the world had had a class like that.

If that was what being a teacher was all about then I wasn't going to be in the profession for very long. I wanted an easier job.

Ian said I could quit the class if I wanted to, but he challenged me to use my own teachings to get through this difficult time. He knew I was writing a self-help book, and here I was, needing the help. The irony! As Fiona would be in on Monday, he suggested I spend the weekend working on my own self-development and see how I felt about the class afterwards. If I still felt the same, then Fiona would be able to find a replacement. But if I felt different, it would help me a lot as a teacher if I continued with the class.

I spent a lot of time visualizing that weekend. I saw myself standing and walking around the class with confidence. I imagined myself speaking with confidence – each word slow, measured, clear and projected with ease. I also did it for real. I stood in power poses and walked with power around my bedroom, pretending I was teaching decimals, ratios and proportions with the utmost clarity and confidence.

By Monday, I did feel a lot more confident. Still afraid, but more confident. And something Ian had said had got into my head, about it being best for my long-term growth if I saw it through to the end. I could turn the whole thing into a self-help lesson for myself. Somehow that made it easier to face.

By the time I arrived at the class on the Thursday I had done so much visualizing, power posing, power walking and power talking, that I automatically moved into that style. There was still a lot of noise and misbehaviour, but I handled it better. It helped that the class was reduced in size, from 20 to 12. Most had been dismissed, for a variety of reasons.

I'm not sure how it came about, but one of the boys asked me a question about my life. I told them I had a PhD in chemistry and had previously worked as a scientist developing drugs. Then I gave them a quick five-minute lesson on what real drugs were – the medicinal kind. I explained that roots and leaves found in rainforests seemed to help people with illnesses like cancer and that the chemical was extracted and given to chemists like me, who then made several of versions of it, tweaking a few atoms here and there, to see if any of them worked better than the root or leaf itself. I gave them a few examples on the blackboard of the kind of alterations we made and why we made them, and explained that one of these would eventually become the white pill that you get from the doctor.

They were amazed. One asked me if I knew about space travel. His dad had told him that *Star Trek* would be reality one day. So I explained that 'warp technology' was actually when you pulled two pieces of space together so the distance wasn't a trillion miles, but just a few yards. I held up a piece of paper, poked a pen through two ends and pulled the paper together so the pen was a bridge. I told them it was called an Einstein-Rosen bridge, after the two professors who figured it out.

I was stunned by how fascinating they found it. 'This is mad shit,' said one boy enthusiastically. They all wanted more. So I made a deal with them: I'd give them 20 minutes of mad shit each time if they gave me their attention for the rest of the lesson.

That's how it went for the next 10 weeks. As well as decimals, ratios and proportions, we covered organic chemistry, quantum entanglement, neuroscience, the placebo effect and many other topics. We even devoted a session to aliens.

It worked. By the end of the course, everyone in the class got an 'A'. I fondly remember handing a marked test paper back to a large tough-looking boy with a deep, gruff voice. As he saw the 'A' in large red writing at the top, he whispered, 'You've given me the wrong paper.'

He'd simply made the assumption that he couldn't possibly get an A. He believed he was *not good enough*.

I assured him it was his paper and that he should be proud of himself. He'd earned his 'A'. His eyes immediately welled up with tears. He quickly looked away, embarrassed.

I walked on, tapped his shoulder and said, 'Well done, son!' I hope that helped him feel that he *was* good enough.

I learned just last year that one of those boys had gone on to university and graduated with a first-class honours degree in engineering.

Magic can sometimes happen when we face our difficulties instead of trying to avoid them. Visualizing and power posing helped me to face this challenge. They rewired my brain sufficiently in the week leading up to the second lesson. I kept the practice up for a few more weeks after that too. It showed me clearly that by changing our brain, and therefore how we respond to life's events, we find new possibilities opening up that quite simply didn't exist for us before.

♥♥♥ 🏋 SELF-LOVE GYM: *How to Be a Self-Love Olympian*

♦ Think of a situation where your self-worth is low. It might be at work, at home, in a social situation, on the telephone. You might be getting bullied or taken advantage of. You might be giving your power away. You might be able to think of many different scenarios...

♦ Now imagine yourself in the same situation but now in a state of 'I *am* enough.' Imagine how you'd be standing. How would you move? Would your spine be erect? What about your shoulders? How would you be breathing? What would you be saying? How would you be saying it? What kind of tone would your words have? Would you speak quickly or slowly?

♦ Play the scene out in your mind five to 10 times as you wire 'I *am* enough' into your brain. Start the first few times by reminding yourself of how you were in the *not* enough stage, but by the third or fourth time, just go straight into imagining your behaviour from an 'I *am* enough' space.

♦ Repeat this process consistently – either daily or a few times a week – until you actually do show you are *enough* in that situation.

Insight to Wired

When I talk about wiring brain networks, sometimes someone comments that surely a person can just have a moment of insight and *know* they are *enough*, just as a person can have a moment of insight that leaves them enlightened.

That's absolutely true! And with that insight come changes in brain chemistry that support the new mindset. Over time, with consistent thinking and feeling in this new way, brain networks build up and wire in that knowledge, and once the brain networks are there, there's very little chance you'll *ever* go back to the *not* enough stage of self-love. Ultimately, it only does take one thought.

If that insight hasn't struck you yet, though, don't despair – keep wiring in 'I *am* enough' and you'll make it stick! Repetition! Repetition! Repetition!

In summary... The brain doesn't distinguish between real and imaginary. Plenty of research shows that it changes as we do something and changes by about the same amount if we imagine doing the thing instead.

All élite athletes use this phenomenon of neuroplasticity to enhance their performance through visualization. Rehabilitation specialists also teach visualization to patients recovering from a stroke, because imagining movement actually helps the brain to recover.

What all this means is that we can imagine ourselves acting with a healthy level of self-worth and our brain will wire in this healthy level.

We can also forget how to have low self-worth, just as we can forget how to do long division. If we don't give our attention to thinking of ourselves as small or less-than and instead focus on thinking and acting in a way that's congruent with healthy self-worth, the brain networks connected with our lack of self-love will simply dissolve.

Part II

What Does It Matter?

'The most common form of despair
is not being who you are.'

SOREN KIERKEGAARD

Chapter 5

Does It Matter If People Like You?

'I'm a rose whether I'm admired or not. I'm a rose whether anyone's crazy about me or not.'

SERDAR ÖZKAN

I spoke at a conference in Las Vegas in 2007, shortly after my first book was published. It felt like my big break and I wanted it to go well. At one point during a story that I was telling, a man in the front row was laughing so hard he fell right off his chair and landed in the aisle, still in hysterics. I saw him and immediately felt on a high.

A split second later, a man on the far left of me also caught my attention. While it seemed that everyone in the auditorium was laughing, he had a bored, stern look on his face. My own face flushed. I lost concentration. If it wasn't for the fact that when people are laughing you can say almost anything and get away with it, I would have crash-landed right there. There were only 10 minutes of my talk left, so even though I stumbled through it, I don't think anyone else noticed.

Later that evening, as we sat having drinks, my partner, Elizabeth, told me how proud she was of me and how people were stopping her and telling her what a great talk I'd given. You'd think I'd be on a high, wouldn't you? I certainly had moments of internal celebration, but my mind kept returning to the man on my left who hadn't been smiling. My face flushed each time I thought of him. I wondered if I'd offended him. I ran through bits of my presentation in my mind, looking for anything that could offend, but I found none. I wondered if he was a university professor or a sceptic who had taken offence to the fact that I bridge mainstream science with self-help, alternative medicine and spirituality. I hoped I wouldn't run into him in case he was aggressive. You know how I was around aggressive people!

As you may gather, this was a time in my life when I was overly concerned with whether people liked me or not. I suspect you've behaved in much the same way in your own life. We are, after all, only human.

Cut Yourself a Little Slack

It's been said that you shouldn't be concerned with whether people like you or not, only with whether *you* like yourself or not.

I like those words and I suspect you do too. There's something comforting in them, something that feels true. Perhaps it's the sense of light at the end of the tunnel.

I think this is why we all like quotes so much. They remind us of wisdom we know but usually forget in our day-to-day life. Words like these give us hope and remind us of who we want to be and how we want to be.

To be unconcerned with what people think of you is a worthy goal to have. But it's also OK to cut yourself some slack and not get annoyed at yourself when you *are* concerned.

It's normal to want people to like you. So long as you're not obsessed with it, it's quite healthy, because it means you'll be aware of your own behaviour. How would the world be if we all just kept on being ourselves with no regard whatsoever for the impact of our behaviour on others?

The key is to have a healthy awareness of how others may perceive us, but not to adopt their opinions as our own unless we can honestly see some truth in them. Some of us get the idea that to be happy, or enlightened, we need to be 100 per cent unconcerned about what people think of us. But living with absolutes like this is only setting ourselves up for not being enough: if we're not 100 per cent free of people's opinions of us, we've failed, or if we don't feel *enough* 100 per cent of the time, we've failed.

But life is not black or white, nor is it something in between. Life kind of floats from black to white and white to black, dances a little on the grey, splurges in yellows and oranges, meditates on the blue, goes wild on the red and is pretty much, for the most part, quite unpredictable. If we can live with that, then great.

If we can live with a concern for what people think of us but not be too bothered when they don't like us, then that's great, too.

I remember the moment I had that insight into my own progress, after working on wiring 'I *am* enough' into my brain for a few months. I was running one of my online courses and after one of my live webinars I received an e-mail from a woman asking for her money back. I don't think she expected me to be answering my own e-mails, because her language was quite clipped as she communicated that she found listening to me really annoying.

It really didn't bother me. My face didn't flush. Instant biofeedback! It showed me that the change I was making was embedded into my brain and nervous system. In the past, on the odd occasion when I'd received some negative feedback, the first thing that happened was that my face flushed and felt hot. This time I didn't need to use any positive self-talk. I didn't need to get angry. I just decided that you can't please everyone and it was a waste of time trying. I just let it go.

I'm telling you about my own transformation here because you'll be able to relate to it yourself. Given you're reading this book, I suspect that, deep down, we're very much the same.

Why We Want People to Like Us

When someone says they don't care what people think of them, most of the time:

1. They're lying.

2. They think they're not very well liked, so their words are more of a coping strategy.

3. They lack confidence around people.

4. What they're saying is an affirmation to help them to get to that place.

There's a reason why we want people to like us. We're genetically wired that way. Our biology needs connection.

We learned long ago that safety came in numbers and that if we helped each other out it was better for all of us. Being rejected meant starvation or death. Even though it doesn't mean that today (except in parts of the world where hunger is a reality), it is still embedded deep in the human psyche. It still brings up the fear at a biological and neurological level. We might not understand the basis for our need to be liked, but we do have that need. It's innate.

So there's absolutely nothing wrong with you if you feel concerned about what people think of you. *Being rejected is the number one human fear. Being accepted is the number one desire.*

Why We're Wired to Connect

Let me share with you a little of how it was that needing to connect and to be accepted came to be innate. The way evolution works is really very simple. It occurs when a gene mutates into two or more versions. It's a bit like two people viewing the same landscape and painting it. Each version, while clearly showing the same landscape, will be slightly different. One person might use lighter shades of colour than the other, for instance.

Let's say a pink gene mutated into a light shade of pink and a darker shade of pink. Now say the gene was a social interaction gene and that the light pink version was one that made a person want to interact with others and the dark pink version was one that made a person not like interaction.

Evolution needs sex to take place. It requires genes to pass from one generation to the next. The person with the lighter pink shade of gene would be more likely to reproduce and pass that gene on to the next generation than the person with the darker shade, because they would be more likely to be out meeting people and forming relationships.

If the light pink gene were four times more likely to be passed on than the dark pink one, what we would find would be that after lots and lots and lots of generations had passed, the light pink gene would be in pretty much every person's genome. Winding the clock forward a half million or so years, not only would the gene now be in every person, but it would also have infiltrated many biological systems, such would be its necessity in the human genome. This is essentially what has happened.

This is why connecting is so healthy and so absolutely necessary for human life. Social connection even acts as a longevity support. Studies of people in their eighties and even over the age of 100 have all found the same thing: that connection is healthy and makes us live longer.

Connecting with one another even helps our mental health. While examining a large social network of over 12,000 people, Nicholas Christakis, formerly a Harvard professor and currently at the Yale Institute of Network Science, and his colleague, James Fowler, from UCLA, found that for every point increase in connectedness, there was a significant increase in happiness.[1]

So, one of the best antidotes to depression is actually to get out and interact with people. It may be hard to do, but it feeds your biology. Sitting at home, isolating yourself, only makes it worse.

In particular, when people enjoy connections, they have healthier hearts. Connection produces the hormone oxytocin, which is a cardioprotective hormone. Basically, that means it protects the heart and cardiovascular system. It lowers blood pressure and also sweeps the arteries clear of some of the precursors to cardiovascular disease. It's a hormone that's essential for human life. The oxytocin gene really is the pink gene I spoke of above. It's so important to evolution that it's estimated to be around 500 million years old. Even dinosaurs needed to connect!

I discussed many of the effects of oxytocin in my book *Why Kindness is Good for You*. Rather than repeat it all here, I recommend you take a look at that book if the subject interests you.

So, deep down, as deep as it goes in fact, we need each other and we want to be accepted and liked by each other. Being accepted and liked goes right to the roots of survival. If we're not accepted or liked, we can't pass our genes on and, essentially, that feels like the end. It's why being rejected is the number one human fear. In the collective human psyche, it's a threat to our very survival.

Why We Shouldn't Compromise Our Authenticity

The fear of not being accepted is so strong it causes both women and men to try to change their appearance to try to be more of what they think the other will prefer.

Deep down, everyone feels that if they look a certain way, they're more likely to be liked, and therefore accepted. Many adjust their behaviour, including how they speak, so that they'll be accepted.

People will do almost *anything* to belong. We've already seen how they will bully to be part of a group and then return to normal once the ringleader has gone. I remember a time at university when many of my fellow students teased a boy because he'd done some things that they deemed to be stupid. When in their company, I joined in. Privately, I felt sorry for him. Did I speak up? Eventually! But I was quickly overpowered by the group and so I joined in again, such was my fear of being rejected. While I've been bullied in my life, I've also been the bully in some ways. We've all done it.

In professional settings, it's quite common for a person to say things they really don't believe, just to stay liked or respected by the group. I once attended a lecture given by a scientist discussing the survival of consciousness after death. He said he'd given the same lecture in the medical department of a large, very well-known university, at a conference held there. During the lecture, the professors gave the impression they didn't believe a word he was saying, but over the few days of the conference, which involved social time, seven professors spoke privately with him and said they agreed with everything he'd said. Some said they'd made observations themselves that indicated the survival of consciousness and had interviewed resuscitated patients. But each asked him not to repeat anything of their conversation to their colleagues, as it could damage their relationship with them and potentially their professional reputation.

The scientist thought it was amusing that each of these professors had the same private thoughts yet maintained the identical charade in their professional lives.

While it makes logical sense for us to run with the crowd, especially if standing alone could harm our career and therefore have a financial impact upon us and our family, on a more primary level, each time we do this we compromise our authenticity and essentially give away a part of ourselves. It's fine to adapt what we say and how we say it out of sensitivity. But not when we do it out of fear. The former says we *are* enough; the latter says we're *not*.

Many people live most of their life on other people's terms, trying to please everyone, always trying to be what others want them to be. They'd like to believe they're just being polite. That's what we tell ourselves, isn't it? But when it comes down to it, most of us are simply afraid of not being liked. If we're not liked, we won't belong. And all of us need to belong. We can tell ourselves that we're happier on our own, but given half a chance to be part of something, we'll jump at it. It's hard to beat biology.

Wanting to be liked is normal, so cut yourself a little slack and don't be hard on yourself when you find yourself trying to please others. The problem arises when you're so afraid of not being liked that you'll compromise your own authenticity to be accepted.

The logic seems sound: be what people want and they'll like you, then you'll be accepted and belong. Great – except that it really doesn't work that way.

Basically, the more we compromise, the weaker our connections and the less we truly feel we belong. The more we're authentic, on the other hand, the higher the quality of our connections and the more we feel we belong. And the more we're our authentic self, the more deeply we wire 'I *am* enough' into our brain networks.

Of course, there are risks involved in being authentic. When you show people your real self, they might not like you. They may reject you. That can be scary. It hits right at the number one fear.

A dear friend of mine who is gay told me that for many gays who haven't come out of the closet, the fear of a negative outcome (i.e. rejection by their family) is still greater than the possible rewards. The rejection, he said, is quite imaginable, and acceptance feels more like a pipe dream.

But what if people do accept you as you really are? In fact, what if they like you even more?

Hard though it can be, we need to focus more on this possibility, lest we remain stuck. Of course it's true that some people could choose to move out of our life. But if that does happen, it leaves space for new people to come in. Wouldn't you rather have people in your life who loved the real you rather than people who liked what you were pretending to be?

It's been said that you shouldn't try to get others to like you. If you're yourself, the right people will come into your life – people who love the real you.

Anaïs Nin wrote, 'And the day came when the risk to remain tight in a bud was more painful than the risk it took to blossom.'

 **SELF-LOVE GYM:** *Being Yourself*

The following exercise is designed to help you to lessen the negative weight of the risks of being authentic and focus more on the possible rewards.

♦ Do you work hard to get people to like you? Who specifically?

♦ Would it ultimately matter if this person/these people didn't like you? What's the worst that could happen?

♦ How might your life and relationships be if you didn't try so hard to get people to like you?

♦ What action could you take that would demonstrate that it didn't matter if someone liked you or not (without being inappropriate or breaking the law)? Remember, it would be a statement of being *enough*.

♦ For the next seven days, do one thing each day that shows that you are more concerned with being yourself than with whether people like you or not. Could you dress the way you want, or do your hair a way that you're worried people (or a specific person) might not like? Could you speak your mind at work and say what you've been afraid to say? Or could you say 'no' when you want to instead of always saying 'yes'?

When she read a draft of this book, my friend Margaret phoned me about the example I gave at the start of this chapter, my talk in Las Vegas. She told me that we couldn't be responsible for how other people perceived us. As long as we did our best, how someone perceived us wasn't up to us, it was up to *them*.

And she was perfectly right. It's not our job to manage people's perceptions of us. We'd be very busy indeed if it were, and we'd quickly be exhausted. We can't please everyone. All we can do is be ourselves.

I've found that if I try to be kind, patient, understanding and sympathetic to others' pain – if I live with personal integrity – then I know that what I'm doing is coming from my heart and it's easier to let go of managing people's perceptions. I know, then, that I'm always doing my best.

I think that if we do this, we'll always feel authentic and always feel that what we're doing and how we're doing it is *good enough*. If people don't like that, that's their problem.

'Mirror, Mirror'

Have you heard about the power of looking in a mirror and saying 'I love you'? Louise Hay has written lots about it and how it helps with self-love. I don't need to regurgitate it here. I'm a fan. I'm converted!

At Louise's 85th birthday party, she gave each guest a little pull-out card with a circular mirror on it stuck in the centre of a heart. Underneath were the words: 'I LOVE YOU.' I have it in my office so I can see it as I write. I've used it often and learned the benefits of the exercise.

The reason I've called this section 'Mirror, Mirror' is because in the course of your self-love project you might think that you don't need to live up to anyone's expectations, you don't need people's approval and that you don't need a specific person or group to like you. That's fine, but other people are perfectly entitled to say the same thing. They don't need to live up to *your* expectations, or need *your* approval, or have *you* like them.

It's important to understand this, because if you do expect people to live their life according to your rules or expectations, or even if you judge them accordingly, you're effectively saying that it's OK for them (or someone else) to be doing the same to you.

In setting yourself free of the expectations, approval and judgements of others, you must set others free of *your* expectation, approval and judgements.

If you find yourself judging others, remember that you can't possibly know what's going on in a person's mind. You can't really know why they're saying what they saying or behaving in the way they're behaving. My mum taught me that growing up and I was reminded of it one morning when I was waiting in line at a coffee shop and a woman drove alongside the queue in a mobility scooter. There was only a narrow space between the line of people and the tables, and she attempted to drive along it. She made it, but drove over my foot in the process. She looked back, but didn't apologize, just carried on.

For a moment I was expecting an apology, but then I just dismissed it and got back to the important task of selecting which pastry I was going to have with my coffee. For the record, I chose a blueberry muffin, which I suppose isn't really a pastry.

The lady and I ended up sitting at adjacent tables. After about half an hour or so, when she'd finished her coffee, she got up and back onto her scooter. It wouldn't start. She tried to turn the key several times, then telephoned the place she'd purchased it from.

An engineer turned up within five minutes. The place must have been local. I couldn't help overhearing what they were saying because they were only a few feet away from me. It turned out the woman had only just collected the scooter that morning. This was her very first outing on it and the first time she'd ever driven a mobility scooter. She'd come to the coffee shop for a rest.

I heard that she felt really self-conscious driving the scooter and wasn't at all confident about it. She certainly wasn't used to its speed, or its width, and this combination made it quite stressful when she had to drive through narrow gaps.

Now I felt such compassion for the lady. Now I realized that when she'd turned round after driving over my foot, she'd probably wanted to say something to me, but a mixture of self-consciousness and embarrassment, plus the fear that she might drive over someone else's foot as she navigated the narrow space between the queue and the tables, had made her channel all her energy into looking forwards and keeping going in a straight line.

It really hadn't bothered me that she'd driven over my foot. But I'd made the assumption that a person driving over another person's foot should apologize and so I'd judged her. That assumption also assumes a level playing field – that everyone has the same degree of stuff going on in their life. But we all know that's not true.

How many times have you felt judged by someone and wished they'd known what your life was like right then? Or what you'd had to weigh up in your mind before making a decision that affected them?

We can't ever know what's going on in a person's mind unless they tell us. So, next time you're about to judge someone, pause for a second and remind yourself that people have judged you without knowing what was going on in your mind or your life. And if you judge others, you invite judgement of yourself.

When you know you *are* enough, you have no need to judge other people. You let them be who they are or who they need to be. That's all.

Remember, we're all just trying to make our way through life with the skills and knowledge that we have. We all have hopes and dreams. And we all get scared. We all have what someone else would think of as a flaw. We all have what others would find beautiful too.

What do you focus on? The beauty or the flaw? It's your choice. What do you see in others? What do you see in yourself?

Practise seeing beauty today. See it in yourself and see it in others.

If you want people to see your beauty, look for theirs.

If you want people to know who you are, show interest in their lives.

♥ SELF-LOVE GYM: *Set Them Free*

Identifying the people you judge and the people you feel judged by helps you to set them free. This in turn helps you to be free – and to move away from *not enough*, especially if you've felt stuck there.

Answer the following questions:

◆ Do you live under the pressure of the expectations of others? Who specifically expects something of you? In what way?

◆ What would your life be like if you were free of these expectations?

◆ What could you communicate to others to free yourself of their expectations?

◆ Could you set anyone free from *your* expectations? What would that mean for them?

◆ What could you communicate to others to free them of your expectations?

In summary... It's natural to want people to like us. It's in our DNA. We're driven to want to connect with others. It feels good. It's also healthy. Good relationships and regular social contact actually prolong lifespan. They also make us happier.

But it's important that we don't compromise who we are to get people to like us. Most of us have the unconscious assumption that if we are what people like, we'll be accepted. But the trouble with compromising our authenticity, which is what we do when we pretend to be something we know we're not, is that we don't ever really get the quality of connection our biology is seeking. The way to get that kind of connection is simply to be ourselves.

Just be yourself: authentic, honest and true to yourself. That's *enough*.

Chapter 6

Shame

'One's dignity may be assaulted, vandalized and cruelly mocked, but it can never be taken away unless it is surrendered.'

MICHAEL J. FOX

'[Shame] … the intensely painful feeling or experience of believing that we are flawed and therefore unworthy of love and belonging.' Sound familiar? That definition comes from shame researcher Brene Brown.

Shame makes it difficult to be our authentic selves because we believe that our authentic selves are flawed. The assumption is that if we show our flawed selves we'll never be accepted. That hits right in the psyche, down in the place that's all about survival. Shame keeps us at *not* enough.

The thing is, shame is just a belief. It's not reality; it's just a belief *about* reality. We need to play a little mental gymnastics with shame to disentangle some thinking.

Extract the 'I Am'

Shame is the belief that we're flawed – damaged, broken, not good enough, and therefore unworthy of love, happiness, connection or belonging.

Shame makes everything personal. It's in the 'I am' that starts the sentence 'I am *not* enough.' It's not that we've done something stupid or that our performance has been poor, or that we've made some bad decisions, it's that we define ourselves as a result of these.

- ◆ Instead of 'I did something stupid', shame says, 'I am stupid.'

- ◆ Instead of 'I did something bad', shame says, 'I am bad.'

- ◆ Instead of 'My body is overweight/untoned/blemished/ ugly, etc.', shame says, 'I am overweight/untoned/ blemished/ugly, etc.'

- ◆ Instead of 'I don't earn enough money to give my family a comfortable life', shame says, 'I am not good/ confident/intelligent enough to earn enough money to give my family a comfortable life.'

- ◆ Instead of 'I have failed', shame says, 'I am a failure.'

The thing is, we are not these things. They are simply circumstances and conditions going on in our life. That's it! There's a world of difference separating 'I did', 'I have' and 'I was' from 'I am'. Make this simple distinction and you can start to build some resilience to shame. I refer to this as 'extracting the "I am"'.

Yes, you might have done the occasional stupid thing. Who hasn't? But that doesn't mean you *are* stupid. Yes, you might feel your body is overweight or blemished, especially when you compare yourself to images in the media, but that doesn't mean that there is something fundamentally wrong with you. It's just how your body feels to you right now in relation to the comparisons you've made. OK, it might be true that you've made a few unfortunate financial decisions (who hasn't?), or failed to act at times when you could have acted to improve your life, but that doesn't make you a failure. It just means that those are the ways in which you've behaved at those times.

We often confuse our behaviour with our identity and the result is shame, which makes it hard to feel worthy. It's easy to think we're a bad person for behaving in a certain way, but *we* are not our behaviour. We've merely *exhibited* certain behaviour – and there may be many reasons for it. Maybe we've experienced hurt or pain in our life, maybe this is all we know, maybe we never learned a different way of interacting with people in the world… Making the distinction between identity and behaviour allows us to accept ourselves while still changing how we are showing up in the world.

SELF-LOVE GYM: *Extracting the 'I Am'*

♦ Write down a list of what you feel ashamed of. The examples above might give you some ideas or it might be something more personal or private to you.

♦ Now rewrite each item on your list in the following five-part form:

1. 'It's not that I am _____ [insert shamer].'

2. 'The truth is that _____ [what you did or how you perceived yourself].'

3. 'That doesn't mean that I am _____ [insert shamer].'

4. 'In fact _____ [insert a positive].'

5. 'I am _____ [insert the opposite].'

Here are a few examples, based on workshop responses, to help you get started:

'[1] It's not that I am stupid. [2] The truth is that I've just done a few things some people might call stupid. [3] That doesn't mean that I'm fundamentally stupid. [4] In fact, I've also made some intelligent choices in my life. [5] I am intelligent.'

'[1] It's not that I am bad with money. [2] The truth is that I've just made a few decisions that turned out not to work as well as I'd hoped. Who hasn't? [3] That doesn't mean I can't manage money. [4] In fact, I've made some very good financial decisions in my life, even if they were small ones. [5] The truth is, I am good with money.'

Notice that this person preferred to write, 'The truth is ...' in part 5. It just felt more like the kind of style he'd use.

'[1] It's not that I am overweight. [2] The truth is that that's only how I've been looking at myself. In some nations, my size would be celebrated. The point is that weight is perception. [3] It doesn't mean that I'm flawed. [4] In fact, some people will find me beautiful. [5] From now on, I'm going to celebrate my beauty.'

Notice that in this example, rather than write 'I am...' for the fifth part this lady simply wrote how she intended to act from then on. It didn't feel right to say that she wasn't overweight. She could understand and appreciate that it was down to perception, and that helped her a lot, but it felt false to say she was an ideal weight or something to that effect. The thought of celebrating her beauty, however, gave her a sense of inner strength and determination. Other people have written 'I am beautiful as I am' or 'I am perfect as I am' or other words to that effect.

◆ Read over your statements every day until you feel that the truth has lodged in your mind.

◆ Add new shamers to your list as they arise and work through them in the same way.

This is another exercise that helps to wire new beliefs into your brain. Even if you feel you've made a breakthrough after the first session, keep reading through your responses for a few more days. Write them all out each time if it helps you. Doing this tightens the weave of the (neural) net, making it stronger.

Four Steps to Shame Resilience

We can also use a little trick of neuroscience to become resilient to shame. The feeling of shame activates the fight-or-flight response in the brain. It's all about self-preservation. Resources then flow towards the stress areas of the brain. While that's happening, it can be difficult to be clear in our mind, to get some perspective, to be honest with others about what we're thinking or feeling... We might not even be able to be honest with ourselves.

The trick is to understand that this is happening. Once we know, we can gently coax our brain into behaving in a different way instead.

So, with this in mind, here are four steps to shame resilience:

Step 1: Diffuse Stress with Insight

For years my mum suffered panic attacks. She told me that it wasn't so much the actual panic attack that she was afraid of, it was the fear of it coming on, especially if she was in a public place. And it was the fear that often brought on the attack.

She once said that if she thought that everyone else in the shopping centre got panic attacks she probably wouldn't get them as much. She would relax, knowing that it was OK if one happened. In other words, the ability not to have a panic attack was in a thought!

Shame is similar in a way. Trying to resist shame can bring it on. Shame makes us feel inadequate. It seems very personal. But if we know that everyone else feels exactly the same way, it weakens the shame. That's the insight. Then the fight-or-flight response isn't activated in the brain. We relax a wee bit.

Shame is natural. It fact it's one of the most natural things about being human. Everybody feels it. Everybody! It's just that most people are afraid to admit it. They're afraid they won't be accepted.

Step 2: Extract the 'I Am'

This is the exercise in reasoning your way around shame that you learned a few moments ago. It's also an exercise in self-compassion, which we'll look at later. As you stop defining yourself by your actions and appearance, you start understanding yourself better. Self-compassion is a natural result.

A key area of the brain for empathy and compassion is called the *insula*. It's halfway between the survival areas, which are active during stress and shame, and the prefrontal cortex, which is the area that controls concentration and helps us focus on thriving. Extracting the 'I am', which fosters empathy and compassion, helps us move from survive to thrive.

Step 3: Dance the Shame Away

This step can actually be quite a lot of fun. It's simply dancing the shame away.

I use a 'victory dance' strategy for a lot of things and one of them is shame. It also helps shunt resources and energy away from the fight-or-flight survival areas of the brain and into empathy and higher-order thinking areas like the prefrontal cortex.

You can use this strategy in two ways:

1. Once you've finished the 'Extract the "I Am"' exercise, you can burst into a little dance, a celebratory dance, a victory dance. Make it light-hearted and positive. Doing this helps attach a positive feeling to your new insights, shifting brain resources all the way to the prefrontal cortex.

2. When you're feeling ashamed about something and you don't feel mentally present enough to diffuse stress with insight or extract the 'I am', just burst into a silly dance.

And it really does have to be a *silly* dance! Keep it up until you either laugh or smile broadly. Believe me, if your dance is silly enough, that won't take long. And let me pass on a little piece of logistical advice to go along with it: make sure you're alone. Lock the door and close the curtains.

In my book *How Your Mind Can Heal Your Body*, I told the story of being caught in a full-on victory dance. It was very embarrassing, but, funnily enough, victory dancing actually got me over the shame. I suppose you want to hear about it now! Well, I used to walk the same route to my 'office' (whichever coffee shop I set up my laptop in) every morning, leaving my house around 6.45 a.m. Around five minutes later I'd reach two connecting underpasses under a road junction. It was a safe bet that I could do a wee dance there. I rarely met anyone at that time in the morning. And I'd usually only dance for a few seconds anyway.

But on one particular morning I lost myself in my moves and danced the entire length of the two underpasses. I was so into it I didn't see what was ahead. And I had my eyes closed as well.

As I opened my eyes at the end of the second underpass, I was met by the uncomprehending stare of a crowd of construction workers, who were standing there in a state of complete bewilderment.

As I mentioned earlier, at moments of high embarrassment or shame, a large part of our brain shifts resources to fight or flight. Intelligent thinking shuts down. You may have noticed that at moments like these you tend to say or do something stupid. I was no different. The only idea I could conjure up was to pretend that my phone was ringing. Only I had no phone in my hand. So I answered my fingers and began to talk loudly to a pretend person.

Unsurprisingly, this only added to the construction workers' assumption that I was crazy. I can't blame them, bearing in mind they'd also just watched me dancing by myself.

However, as you know, victory dancing also got me over the shame. I recalled the thoughts and feelings of shame by replaying the scenario in my mind. Then, once I was cringing with embarrassment, I burst into my victory dance. I only had to do this about 10 times consecutively to actually find the whole thing amusing! The power of victory dancing helped me swiftly to turn shame into a smile.

So, devise your own victory dance and practise it. Do it 10 times in a row, either at the moment of shame or afterwards in the privacy of your own home. By the time you reach the fourth or fifth time, you'll have a much harder time focusing on the thoughts and feelings of shame. This is because your brain will already be learning to send resources away from the stress areas and towards the positive areas. Keep it up for the 10 anyway. Repetition is key when you're rewiring brain networks, as you know.

In some ways it's like speeded-up psychotherapy. One of the ways psychotherapy works, at a neurological level, is that we process a memory from a more positive, often adult, perspective.

Although it's a talk therapy, part of its power is that through talking, our brain networks stop connecting the event to stress and negative emotion and rewire to connect it to a more positive set of insights and emotions, essentially moving resources from stress areas to the prefrontal cortex.

Step 4: Reach Out

It's OK to admit that we feel ashamed or embarrassed. Everyone feels that way sometimes. Reaching out to others can bring us some closure and also give others a chance to be compassionate and perhaps to be honest with us, too.

This is where some magic can happen. In the space of telling someone else how we feel, or how we have been feeling, whether it's a loved one, friend or even a support group, we begin to feel connected. And through connection we come to know that we are *enough*.

Here's a summary of the four steps to shame resilience:

1. Diffuse stress with insight.

2. Extract the 'I am'.

3. Dance the shame away.

4. Reach out.

Shrink It Down

One of the many things Oscar has taught me is to take myself much less seriously. This is because he's done quite a few stupid things. He's fallen down holes, somersaulted when trying to pick up a tennis ball while running at full speed, run out in front of cars, jumped up on a park attendant and tried to grab his 'stick', spotted a bird and dragged me headfirst right through a large group of extremely prickly bushes, much to the amusement of onlookers, and many, many other daft things. At puppy-training classes, the trainer, a former Crufts dog show obedience winner, started to call him 'Marley', after the book and film *Marley & Me*, about another crazy yellow Labrador.

Had Oscar been a human he'd have gone over some of these antics in his mind again and again, well after the events had passed, gradually moving towards feeling embarrassment and shame. He'd think, *I can't believe I did that. And people saw me. Oh, the shame of it.*

But Oscar doesn't feel shame. He wakes up every morning with the biggest grin on his face, tail wagging furiously when he sees me or Elizabeth. The previous day is behind him. The new day has just begun and it's about to be a good one as he looks around for toys to play with or rip apart, or perhaps contemplates the next piece of mischief he can get up to.

We need to be like Oscar. I don't mean that we should run out into roads or launch ourselves on park attendants of course, but we need to get out of the way of our own life. So much of the pain we feel is down to our interpretation of events and our perception of ourselves and what we imagine people think of us. We attach our identity and self-worth to events and then, if they don't work out in the way we want, we judge ourselves. 'I am so _____!'

Oscar has taught me to lighten up. Yes, I can do seemingly stupid things, but can't we all? And I don't do them *all* the time... It doesn't mean I'm stupid. It means I'm normal.

To Oscar, seemingly embarrassing or painful moments are small. To humans, they are huge. Herein lies another powerful way to reduce the pain of shame. Here's what to do:

SELF-LOVE GYM: *Shrinking It Down*

As you know, your brain doesn't distinguish between real and imaginary. So, think of an event that was embarrassing for you. Now shrink it down! Seriously, imagine it getting smaller. You can even use your hands to shrink it down. Imagine the scene shrinking smaller and until it's insignificantly small. Shrink the sound down as well until it's no more than a faint squeak. Your brain interprets this as the event becoming less significant.

Significant events are large in our minds. They feel real and we can imagine them in great detail, usually in rich colour and sound. Less significant events are harder to recall in detail. The bigger and richer an event is in your mind, the bigger its meaning is to you.

So, shrink those shameful events down! You're not ignoring them. You're not pretending they didn't happen. You're just teaching your brain that they mean less to you.

You might have to do this several times for the same event for it to stick. But once you do, the event will have much less of an emotional impact on you.

We Can Be *Enough* without Nee
Be Perfect

Shame sometimes grows out of perfectionisr.
has been defined as 'the tendency to set ex
standards, to rigidly adhere to these standards, a   engage
in overly critical self-evaluations'. Taken to unhealthy extremes,
it's a black-and-white, win-or-lose, all-or-nothing mentality that's
a recipe for unhappiness, low self-esteem and depression.

Don't get me wrong – perfectionism can be healthy. Some
perfectionists merely strive for excellence. But if perfectionism
stems from the belief 'If I'm not perfect, I won't be accepted',
every attempt to be perfect only makes the statement: 'I'll be
enough *when* ...' And each time we define *when*, we push
enough further away. *Enough* becomes a carrot on a stick.

Perfectionists are hyper-sensitive about other people's opinions,
so they often hold back from showing their creations to the world
until they are perfect. 'It needs to be a little bit better before I
can show it' is a common mantra. What they're really saying is, '*I
need to be a little better before I can show myself.*'

They hold back because they think others will be as critical
about them as they are of themselves. The assumption is that
everyone else will see the same inadequacies, failures, bumps
and wobbly bits that they see in themselves.

This prevents them from being seen. It prevents them from
expanding. It ensures that they are less connected with the
world. They shrink back from the world ... and their sense of
self-worth shrinks with them.

any readers of this book will not be perfectionists, but if this does describe you, write down the following affirmation:

'I am not my accomplishments and creations. Regardless of whether I win or lose, succeed or fail, the truth always remains that I am enough.'

You may be surprised by how useful affirmations can be. This is because they help to focus your intention.

As you move forward with your self-love project, you will find unhealthy perfectionism disappears. Healthy perfectionism might remain, as you might be inspired to strive for excellence. And you might find that your environment, your products, your creations, become more beautiful than you imagined possible, because you're operating from a different space. Why not try it?

Go Out and Connect as Yourself

My friend Margaret often tells the story of watching me and a group of my friends being presented with a peace flame for the work we were doing with the charity that we'd set up, Spirit Aid Foundation. She decided then that she had to meet me.

Seemingly by chance, we found ourselves partnered together a few months later on a meditation retreat in India, as the only two representatives from Scotland. We became instant friends.

One of the many things I've learned from Margaret is the power of interacting with people. Margaret talks to everyone. Everyone! And it doesn't matter if they don't speak the same language – she'll find some way of communicating.

After that trip, we ran several workshops together. Margaret had trained as a laughter therapist with a man who came to be her friend, Dr Patch Adams, of the movie of the same name, whose character was played by the late Robin Williams. So we'd travel to events together and she would dress as a clown for the whole trip. She attracted some looks, I can tell you.

One time we were doing a workshop for a large insurance company. We entered the lift to go to the directors' floor. It was occupied by two men in grey suits. They both immediately stared at the floor, clearly uncomfortable, probably due to the fact that Margaret was dressed in clown attire.

I became uncomfortable too, when Margaret began interacting with them. They clearly didn't want to interact at all. The lift floor was much more interesting to them. Margaret was pushing them right out of their comfort zones.

'What's so nice about the floor?' she asked. 'Why don't people talk to each other in lifts? Let's talk. Tell me about yourselves.' She spoke in a playful yet kind way. I felt quite embarrassed, though. Her words were as much for me as they were for the grey men.

But by the time we reached our floor, the men had completely loosened up. One of them was actually loosening his tie as he stepped out, his face flushed. They were both smiling as they left the lift. Job done, as far as Margaret was concerned. I could tell they'd enjoyed the trip in the lift. It had been unexpected, but, damn, it had been a breath of fresh air.

It had been a lesson for me too. If it hadn't been for Margaret, I would have gone up those 30 or so floors also staring at the ground. And why? I would have been self-conscious! Embarrassed! Worried I wouldn't know what to say. Thinking people wouldn't want to interact. Assuming people would want me to mind my own business. Feeling vulnerable. Feeling I'd run out of conversation. Feeling shame. I could go on. Do you recognize any of those feelings?

Even though opportunities to connect continually present themselves to us, we hold back, thinking that if we are our authentic selves we won't be accepted. Yet connection is what we all biologically crave. What's happening?

It can be presented in the form of an equation:

Hold back bits of myself = I'll get connections = I will know I am enough.

The reality is:

Hold back bits of myself = True connection is not possible = I reinforce I am not enough.

So herein lies the simple solution. It really is simple. Here it is:

Go out and connect with people. And connect as yourself!

Margaret taught me to interact with people on purpose. And it's made a real difference in my life. If ever I feel alone, I don't need to stay feeling alone, I can go out and connect with people. I've experienced depression a few times in my life. Connection brought me out of it. It brings you to life when you do it. It brings others to life, too.

So, don't wait for connections to happen to you. Talk to people. Interact with people in shops, supermarkets, on the street. Talk to your neighbours. Talk to your postman. Meet people. Join a group or a club. Volunteer for a charity. Take a class at college. Learn to dance. Learn a language. Make it your mission to connect with people. Set it as your intention and go out and do it. And do it as *yourself*. Your real self. If you do, you'll start to feel connected.

And because connection is connected, so to speak, with a state of being *enough*, you will also start to know that you *are* enough.

In summary... Everyone feels shame. It's a normal human emotion. There's little use trying to resist it, just as there's little use trying to resist occasionally feeling unhappy. But we can learn to become resilient to shame, just as we can learn to move through unhappiness.

We learn shame resilience by first understanding that we're not alone in feeling shame. Part of the pain of shame is thinking it's personal.

The second step is learning to extract the 'I am' – to separate our identity from our actions. For instance, we can rephrase 'I am stupid' into 'I did something stupid.' This simple turnaround gives birth to hope, because we move away from the feeling that we're fundamentally flawed and towards identifying behaviour that we can change.

The third step uses a little trick of neuroscience to shunt brain resources in moments of shame towards areas that are associated with positive emotion. In other words, dance!

The fourth step of shame resilience is to reach out and connect with people while being honest and authentic. This gives connection – and self-love – a real chance to grow.

Chapter 7

Body Image

*'The reason we struggle with insecurity
is because we compare our behind-the-
scenes with everyone else's highlight reel.'*

STEVE FURTICK

'I can only be happy if I accept what I look like from this day onwards.'

Those were the words of a young woman who attended one of my 'I ♥ Me' workshops. She was talking about the pressure many young women feel under to be slim, have clear skin and have small hips. She said the pressure bred dissatisfaction.

'Accepting what I look like is my only hope,' she explained. 'I'm never going to be like that, so there's no point in trying. If I try, I'm only going to be even unhappier with the way I look.'

Her words were met with nods of support from the other workshop participants. One of them tried to encourage her by saying that she was beautiful as she was.

'But you miss my point,' she replied. 'I need to *not care* whether I'm pretty or not. I want to like myself just as I am.'

Does that sound familiar? It's something we'd all love: to like ourselves (not even love ourselves, just like) as we are. We'd be free.

'How do you do it? How do you get there when the world tells you different? I'm fat,' another woman said, making an open-armed gesture with one finger of each hand pointing at her waist. 'Everyone knows that's not pretty.'

Someone else said, 'You need to find what is pretty about yourself.'

The woman got emotional at that point. For her, it just didn't feel possible to find something about herself that was pretty.

This is such a common feeling. I meet lots of people who would be unable to find anything they liked about themselves.

From this perspective, learning to love yourself feels like having a mountain to climb, but like all mountains, it starts with small steps. In this chapter, I'd like to offer you some small steps that might help change how you feel about your body image.

Love the Skin You're In

The vast majority of women have dieted. A UK study estimated it as 87 per cent of the female population.[1] I have three sisters. Each of them, and my mum, has dieted on numerous occasions. When quizzed, most women say it's to be slim and to increase their self-confidence and self-esteem. That's the answer my mum gives too.

Body image is in fact the number one Major Shamer. Whether it is because of weight, shape, thighs, tummy, breast size (in women), penis size (in men), body hair, going bald (in men), skin blemishes or something else, most people feel self-conscious and insecure about and want to change at least one part of their body.

It might come as little surprise to know that shame about body image plays a role in eating disorders. In a 2014 study, researchers compared 46 people with an eating disorder with 50 healthy participants and another 22 people who had recovered from an eating disorder. Those with the eating disorders were found to have the highest levels of shame.[2]

Shame was also higher in those who had recovered from the eating disorders, which might suggest that whatever way they'd managed to recover, they hadn't dealt with the issue of shame. It's the same reason why many people yo-yo diet. While a diet might help us lose weight, if it doesn't deal with the issues of shame and self-worth, there's always a chance we'll gain weight again.

Learning self-love involves learning to be comfortable with ourselves as we are. It doesn't mean we won't ever want to change. Change is natural. Self-love, in fact, usually does inspire positive, healthy change.

My partner, Elizabeth Caproni, is an actress and filmmaker. She knows all too well the pressures on women. She entered a competition to promote positive body image as part of a campaign called 'Body Gossip', the brainchild of actress and puppeteer Ruth Rogers.

Elizabeth's short monologue/poem is about the transition from *not* enough through *had* enough to *am* enough. It's about being comfortable with yourself. It was one of the winners and was performed by celebrities in front of audiences around the UK, including one containing the Duchess of Cornwall, the wife of Prince Charles. You can find a recital performed by UK celebrities on YouTube.[3]

Here is the poem:

Mocha Choca Latte, Yah Yah ... Please

Yah, I'll have a decaf extra skinny mocha choca latte please.
My waist will be smaller to accentuate my double Ds!

You see that's the only part of me that's allowed to be big.
Otherwise the press will have a field day and call me a pig.

They papped me on holiday, lying in the sun,
Then proclaimed to the world, 'Ha, look at her bum!'

In a terrible state I rushed to the gym,
Pleading my trainer, 'Please make me thin!'

The next two weeks I was worked to the bone,
My ass, thighs and abs ordered to tone.

My dairy became soya and steak became fish.
The pounds were dropping off, I was getting my wish!

I grabbed my trainer and said, 'You're my hero!
I've dropped 3 dress sizes, I'm now a size zero!'

On top of the world, I attended a première,
Expecting the press to say, 'Wow, what a derrière!'

Instead, though, they didn't, and this is what I read,
'She looks like a rake and has a lollipop head.'

Shocked and confused, just what the hell do they want?!
I thought I'd be praised for looking skinny and gaunt.

What, I get slagged for being fat and for being thin?
Well, I give up, I don't know how to win.

Now young girls are starving to look like me,
Viewing my airbrushed pictures, if only they could see

That I have blemishes, lumps and bumps just like them.
See, if they could see that, well, maybe then

Things could change and we'd be allowed to be free,
No dangerous diets and starving, but we could just be

Whatever size we naturally are
And we'll be admired from close-up and afar.

They say that beauty is in the eye of the beholder,
We should believe this, instead of looking over our shoulder

At who is thinner, prettier and whose bones stick out most
It's time to take a stand, I don't wanna be a ghost!

When will we be happy with what we see in the mirror?
We are beautiful – let's stop getting thinner and thinner!

You know what, forget what I ordered – for goodness' sake
I'll have a full-fat latte – and a carrot cake!

A healthy balanced diet with a few treats thrown in
That's the way to go – that's the way to win!

So what if I have a few dimples on my thighs,
It's about time that magazines stopped telling lies.

I'm taking a stand and being happy, not just thin.
It's time to be content with the skin that I'm in.

Average Joe or GI Joe?

Although most of this chapter so far has been about women, men experience similar pressures. It's just not as obvious or talked about.

Highly toned male models are now commonplace in male advertisements. And between the 1970s and 2000, the average *Playgirl* centrefold male gained 26lb (12kg) of muscle and lost around 11lb (5kg) of fat.[4]

Just as women and young girls are dieting, a growing number of men and young boys have been taking action in the opposite direction. In 2014, the UK Home Office reported that steroid use is now so widespread that they estimate around 60,000 people in the UK inject themselves with steroids each year.[5] Research teaches us that a large number of teenage boys are taking steroids because they think they're puny. Just as women compare themselves to ideal images in magazines, online and in the media, so boys do the same, and as a result, they feel under pressure to be more muscular.

Yet again what lies behind this, for both girls and boys, is the pressure to be what they think is attractive, so they can connect and belong. They get the impression that thin and pretty (girls)/ toned and muscular (boys) are normal and what everyone prefers to look at. If they attain the desired shape, they'll be liked, they'll be accepted and ultimately they'll feel they're *enough*. In the meantime, they can become stressed about changing their body image to fit the norm to the point where they end up ignoring what's good about themselves and only seeing what they think are faults. I know what that's like from when I was a teenager.

In the early to mid-eighties, hair was the big thing for boys. The idols when I was a teenager were Morten Harket from the Swedish band A-Ha, and Jason Donovan, who at the time was an actor in the Australian soap *Neighbours*, alongside Kylie Minogue. Both had well-groomed hair that was parted at the front and had three or four inches of length at the back, kind of like a mullet only the hair was straight.

I spent hours trying to get my hair to look just like theirs. When it wouldn't sit just right, I felt embarrassed. If the front didn't sit up as it was supposed to, I would even walk around all day at school with my head down to reduce the risk of people seeing it, or avoid eye contact in the hope that people wouldn't notice me. I could only see what was wasn't right and completely missed everything that was. Nowadays, we call this kind of thing body dysmorphia, though it usually relates to body size and shape, not hair.

Although the pressures are different now from how they were in the eighties, the issue is the same. Young boys and men, just like young girls and women, attach their self-worth to their body image and believe that if they don't look a certain way, people won't like, love, be attracted to or accept them.

Man Up

As a man, I can also tell you that we live with another, less obvious pressure. We need to appear strong, not just in the muscle department but emotionally. We need to 'man up' whenever the situation calls for it.

This pressure leads to all sorts of bravado behaviour. If we didn't do it, we'd be comparing penis sizes instead. The truth is, we feel weak some of the time. For some men, it's a lot of the time. We feel weak about a lot of things. We get scared but feel we're not supposed to, we sometimes feel bad about our inability to provide, we sometimes feel inferior in relation to our sexual performance, especially if we know our wife or partner has been with other men before us. That's a big one for a lot of men, if you pardon the pun. We also worry that we don't look toned or groomed enough, especially when we compare ourselves with other men and learn than women like toned, well-groomed men. We also get emotional and we know that's not allowed.

At the risk of shattering the illusion some women have that men are naturally strong, a lot of men cry from time to time. We'd never admit it, though, not to women, and definitely not to other men. Of course, being a *real* man, I'm not talking about myself here. Just other men I've read about, of course. Ahem…

I don't know any men who, on a first date, will say, 'You know, I had such a good cry last night. Wow, it was good!' Our fear is the next thing we'll hear is a 'whoosh' sound and the distant click of our date's heels getting into a cab.

But emotions are as natural for men as they are for women. Some men suppress theirs, but that has its consequences. Either they stay quiet and live a life feeling that part of them is dead or dying, or the emotions burst out from time to time, sometimes in a display of erratic or stupid behaviour or sometimes in the form of bullying, abusive behaviour. The aggression helps keep the emotion down.

All in all, there's a stereotype that we feel we need to live up to. It's someone who is strong, toned, well groomed, in control of his emotions, sexual dynamite and a good breadwinner.

For men, part of self-love is accepting ourselves as we are – completely, not just the way we look. That doesn't mean we won't ever want to change. In fact, self-love usually does inspire creative change.

Which leads to…

Should You Diet?

Diets help people to look different. And many people do feel much better about their new image. But if we imagine that we'll only be *enough* when we lose x pounds or reach a size y, we're saying that we're *not* enough now. And that's where the problem lies.

As long as we're saying we're *not* enough now, every action we take further compounds the idea that we're *not* enough. So, when we're on a diet, although there will be weeks when the pounds drop off through sheer determination, the weight of the belief that we're *not* enough is likely to see them all put back on again. Each time there's progress, there's a piece of elastic pulling us back, an irresistible urge to eat cake, the thought of just having a takeaway this one last time, or even finding ourselves in the company of people who'd prefer to see us eating the way we always did. They're used to us like that, after all.

If we do reach our ideal weight, because it was motivated by a lack of self-love, the new weight doesn't solve the problem. The sentiment of *not* enough usually runs so deep that a change in appearance is only a temporary sticking plaster that washes off the first time we step in the shower.

To make weight-loss stick, we need to rewire our brain with 'I *am* enough … *now*!'

Many women resist working on self-love, however, because they fear that if they love themselves, they won't care anymore what people think and will just let their body go to pot. This comes up as a genuine concern for some women at 'I ♥ Me' events.

But here's the thing: self-love won't stop you dieting. You won't suddenly become so satisfied with your body that you won't care what anyone thinks and will just gorge yourself on cakes and cheese. It *could* happen, but that's more likely to be a short-term effect of the state of '*I've* had *enough*.'

As you move to '*I* am *enough*' it's actually far more likely that you *will* diet. But you'll do it for different reasons. You'll do it because you're motivated to make healthy choices. It's the same, but it's completely different!

Four Steps to Feeling Better about Your Body Image

Here are four steps that can help you to feel better about your body image and accept yourself as you are.

Step 1: Decide to Get There!

Decide that you are going to learn to like yourself as you are.

That decision doesn't take you there right away. You're not deluding yourself. It just gives you a direction to head in.

It doesn't mean you want to stay as you are. That can be a stumbling block for some people, as we've already seen. 'If I accept myself as I am then I won't lose weight', for instance, is the belief. And such is the desire to lose weight that you are prevented from accepting yourself. But acceptance actually causes spontaneous change. This is what I call the *acceptance paradox*.

The acceptance paradox is that once acceptance arrives, whatever you accept begins to change. Naturally. Complete acceptance produces spontaneous change. It often leads to a spontaneous desire to be healthy or to engage in behaviour that makes you happier.

It also means that any change will originate from a state of *enough* rather than *not* enough.

Step 2: Understand that Opinions are Subjective

We all live under a lot of pressure to conform to the latest styles, to force our body to become thinner and not show any visible signs of ageing. To be attractive, in short.

However, opinions really are subjective. And they change. Opinions about what's attractive are as changeable as the Scottish weather. Right up until the twentieth century, an ideal woman was plump. You can tell by looking at the most common shape in the paintings of nude or almost-nude women painted in the eighteenth and nineteenth centuries. Plump was attractive. Plump was sexy. A plump woman would feel good about herself. She could feel she could walk down the street with her head held high, knowing that male heads would turn everywhere she walked.

But if that woman lived today, she could well be depressed. She would almost certainly be self-conscious about her weight. She would look at women, especially in magazines and in online advertising, who are considered attractive, and she would compare them to herself and feel ugly. Her head wouldn't be quite as high as she walked down the street. Maybe she'd wear trousers instead of a skirt because she felt ashamed to show her legs.

In the 1920s, the vital statistics of the average Miss America winner were 32–25–35. In the 1930s, they were 34–25–35, an average of two inches larger-busted. The stats were 35–25–35, larger-busted again, in the 1940s. A 1920s winner wouldn't even have made the finals in the 1940s. In the 1950s, bust and hip size became larger and waist size shrank. The average stats were 36–23–36.[6]

Had the female size changed in this short span of time? Evolution is not quite so fast! What changed was opinion, strongly influenced by fashion and advertising and by the current leading lady in the movies.

The twenties' view of the ideal woman was influenced by flapper fashion, which incidentally was the result of the first mass-market magazines that used photographs of models rather than hand-drawn images. Models were chosen so the clothes would look as though they were on coat hangers. Wind the clock forward to the 1950s and Marilyn Monroe was a big star. Consequently, most Miss America winners then were around the same size as she was.

Since the 1990s, the popular beauty ideal has been the waif model – heroin chic. Some sociologists believe this has played a significant role in the large increase in eating disorders in young girls and women.

And to top it all off, most advertising images nowadays are airbrushed. So not only do you have to be slim, but you have to have unblemished skin, oh, and be free of cellulite, too.

The trouble with this is that we all suffer by comparison. Research clearly shows that when women look at images of other women in adverts and in the media, it makes them feel dissatisfied with their own body and lowers their self-esteem.

For instance, in a 2009 study, 299 French and Italian girls of an average age of 20 were shown 'idealized' images of seemingly beautiful women in magazines and were found to be dissatisfied with their own body afterwards.[7] Hundreds of similar studies offer the same conclusion.

And where you live matters, too. In some countries, Mauritania for example, large women are celebrated as beautiful. Women there are actually encouraged to put on weight. If a size zero model lived there she might be thought to be the least attractive person in the village.

Our minds are swayed on a daily basis regarding what is attractive. In a 2014 study, some people were shown images of plus-sized models and others images of underweight models for only one minute. Then they were shown images of women of different sizes. Those who had viewed the plus-sized models found a BMI of 18.4 the most attractive, but those who were shown the underweight models preferred a BMI of 16.9.[8]

The point isn't so much the actual BMI but the difference in the BMIs that were found to be attractive. What we are shown in newspapers and magazines, on billboards and online, conditions us to view certain sizes and looks as beautiful and others as not. The same person might be pretty one week, ugly the next, and back to pretty again, all depending on what we have seen in the media during that span of time. We might think that we're in control of our own minds, but they are swayed far more than we think.

Coming to the realization that opinions are subjective is important. It frees us from linking self-worth to body image.

SELF-LOVE GYM:
Convince Me That Opinions Are Subjective and Change

As an exercise, write a few paragraphs as if you were teaching someone else that opinions are subjective and change. Write a page if you feel like it – it's up to you. Do whatever it takes to get it clearer in your own mind.

To make a start, why not reread the section above, highlight the pieces that resonate most with you and make some notes. You can even do some more research online if you feel moved to. With your notes to hand, write as if you were making a case. You might even find it helps to talk over the subject with a friend.

I often use exercises like these. They are very powerful. When you teach someone else what you've learned, it brings you new insights and a richer understanding of the subject.

Step 3: Allow Yourself to Be a Square Peg in a Round Hole

So now you know that opinions are subjective and change, you don't need to try to be like everyone else. Opting to be authentic as yourself (which might be different from others in some ways) can be a statement that you feel you're *enough*. Celebrate your uniqueness!

♟ SELF-LOVE GYM: *Celebrate Your Uniqueness*

♦ Write down how comparing yourself to others has affected, and is affecting now, your happiness, health and feelings of self-worth.

♦ Next write down how your life could be different if you stopped comparing yourself to others and instead began to accept yourself as you are. For example, if comparing yourself to others is making you feel insecure, how do you think you would feel if you stopped making the comparison? Would you feel more secure? How would that affect your relationships, your career, your health, your finances, etc?

♦ Make a decision to be your unique self. Try it for a day. Wear what you want to wear. Speak your mind. Be yourself as a living affirmation that you are *enough*.

Step 4: Focus on What You Like about Yourself

A girl who attended one of my workshops shared this exercise with me. It was taught to Japanese women with low self-esteem and massively improved it, moving many of the women all the way from low self-esteem to healthy self-esteem. It's also been shown to be effective in research studies.

🏋️ SELF-LOVE GYM: *What Do You Like about Yourself?*

♦ Choose three parts of your body you like. Maybe it's your hair. Or perhaps it's your feet. Or something in between! Maybe it's your voice, or your eyes, or your skin.

♦ Focus on these three parts every day for the next week. You might feel like accentuating them or you might just allow yourself to reflect on why you like them. Whatever you choose to do, keep doing it. It's the consistency of focusing on these body parts that makes the exercise so powerful.

Here's a summary of the four steps to feeling better about your body image:

1. Decide to get there.

2. Understand that opinions are subjective and change.

3. Allow yourself to be a square peg in a round hole.

4. Focus on what you like about yourself.

As with many of the exercises in this book, the work is like going to the physical gym: the biggest breakthroughs come when you're consistent. With body image, that means going over your responses to the questions on a few different occasions and even adding something new each time you do.

Some of you will need to do more reps of the exercise than others. You might have to do an exercise three times a week for two weeks to see some real benefit. But, just like the physical gym, it's always worth putting the work in.

In summary... Most of us feel unhappy about some aspect of our body image; whether it's our weight, shape, skin, cellulite, nose, teeth, hair, breast size (women), hip size (women) or penis size (men). What drives this is the unconscious belief that we need to be better – more attractive – to be accepted. But opinions on what is 'perfect' are subjective and they change. In fact, an 'ideal' body shape 100 years ago would be considered overweight today. And an overweight person in some countries today would be considered slim in another.

There are four powerful steps you can take to feel better about your body image and accept yourself as you are.

Some people face a dilemma when it comes to accepting themselves as they are. They so want to change that they don't want to accept themselves. But accepting yourself is an important part of self-love. This is where the acceptance paradox comes in: once acceptance arrives, whatever you accept begins to change.

Self-acceptance usually gives birth to inspired, creative change and it does so from 'I *am* enough' instead of *not* enough.

Chapter 8

Vulnerability

'Being deeply loved by someone gives you strength, while loving someone deeply gives you courage.'

Lao Tzu

I met a homeless man in London early one Sunday morning. Our brief exchange left a lasting impression upon me.

I had just left a hotel with the intention of travelling to King's Cross station to catch a train home to Scotland when I passed the man on the street. He was carrying what seemed to be his worldly belongings in a cluster of carrier bags, two or three to each hand. He looked so very sad and tired, and was walking slowly.

I walked on, but part of me couldn't forget him. When I reached the street corner, I looked into a café, where people were sitting in the warmth, protected from the cold. I thought of going in to grab a coffee. As I stood there, about to open the door, I glanced back and watched the man shuffle slowly across the street. I felt as though I was looking in two windows at once. In one were the warmth of the coffee shop and the taste of freshly ground coffee. In the other was the homeless man, alone on this cold, damp Sunday morning, with nowhere to go to keep warm.

I went back. I crossed the street and found him sitting down in a shop doorway. I'd thought he was around 60 years old, but up close he looked about the same age as me, only aged by loneliness and cold. I placed £10 in his hand. What happened next has left an imprint on my soul.

Looking up at me, he made a prayer sign of thanks with his hands. He said nothing, but he didn't need to: never have I witnessed such gratitude in a person's eyes. His were a piercing blue, reminding me of those of Jesus of Nazareth in the movie of that name. He seemed holy in that moment, completely vulnerable, special. I, on the other hand, felt ashamed and small. Should I have given him more?

I realized that he saw himself as beneath me. In his view, I and others could choose to bestow upon him money or food as we saw fit and could somehow decide his fate.

I walked away, fighting back tears. I thought angrily, No, you are not beneath me, dear sir. You are not beneath anyone! You have a right to happiness.

I said a prayer for him and imagined him knowing his worth and finding happiness. It made me feel a little better, even though I still wish I could meet him again and do more for him.

When we show our vulnerability, others see our greatness. As I blended back into the crowd, not showing mine, hiding among the hundreds of people going about their lives, many also pretending, I felt small and weak. In that simple exchange, the homeless man was most definitely the better man.

You see, I have come to measure greatness in the courage to bare one's soul. He showed his. I hid mine behind my wallet and my nice clothes. I chose not to show any emotion as I offered that small sum. I chose not to say anything. I simply smiled, touched his hand lightly, stood up and walked away. He, on the other hand, showed complete openness. I think that's why he penetrated through my guard so much. He was completely vulnerable. There was absolutely no pretence, just 100 per cent authenticity. In that moment, he was *enough*. I wasn't.

It's hard not to be shaken to your core when someone shows real authenticity and vulnerability, especially when it contrasts so much with your own space. We're so unused to it that when it happens it almost knocks us off our feet. But vulnerability is the doorway to love, friendship and lasting relationships. It's the doorway to a sense of connection and belonging. It's the doorway to being *enough*.

The homeless man's authenticity and vulnerability affected me so much I still feel the connection to him. It's why I've been moved to write about it in this book. Even though we might never meet again, we will be connected forever. His vulnerability facilitated that.

It also ensured that his soul has now touched the lives of countless people reading this book. That's the power of vulnerability.

The Power of Vulnerability

Being vulnerable doesn't mean that we need to be an open book and bare our soul to everyone we meet. But it does invite us to let our guard down.

And it has to be authentic. Some people open up to get attention, but they do it to get people to like them. That's not real vulnerability. Real vulnerability can only be authentic. If it's not authentic, it's not vulnerable. Anyone can tell the difference.

Vulnerability demands honesty with ourselves and honesty with others. It takes courage. But that courage says, 'I *am* enough.'

Sure, it can be scary. We're saying, 'This is who I am. It doesn't matter whether you accept me or not. Here I am anyway.' And there's always a chance that we won't be accepted. But when we're true to ourselves, that really doesn't matter at all. In those fleeting moments, somewhere deep down we know that being true to ourselves is *enough*.

Authenticity and vulnerability both equate to *enough*. We needn't hide in case someone sees the real us. And showing other people who we really are is the pathway to connection.

Of course this means being honest with ourselves. It means accepting our imperfections and not hiding them. It means being honest with others. It means not holding back. It means showing how we feel. It means risking rejection. It means stepping out of our comfort zone. It means being vulnerable.

We show vulnerability when we write, build, create a product or perform and put what we do or have created out into the world for people to see, knowing that they might not like it ... or us.

We're vulnerable when we have to have difficult conversations with our partner, children or co-workers.

We're vulnerable when we initiate sex, knowing that we might be rejected.

We're especially vulnerable when we choose to love someone completely, even though we know we might get hurt.

Vulnerability is asking an employer for what we need, even though they might say no.

It's admitting that we're afraid, knowing that people might think we're weak.

It's being honest about feeling sad when people expect us to be happy.

Part of my personal vulnerability in this book is sharing some of my own weaknesses. When you've written seven previous books in the self-help field, people expect you to be whole and wise, to have all the answers and certainly not to have any personal problems. When I started writing this book, I thought people would be asking, 'How can a person with personal difficulties write a self-help book?' I was afraid they wouldn't hold me in the same esteem as before. Maybe they'd stop coming to my talks because they'd think I wasn't as 'healed' as other authors. I was even afraid that I wouldn't have anything significant to say and that no one would want to read a self-love book written by a man.

Those were the things – risks, I suppose – that swam around in my mind. But I actually felt relief as soon as I began allowing audiences to learn how I've stumbled through my life at times, how I've had to feel my way in the dark, how I've struggled and still struggle.

What I didn't expect was people telling me that they appreciated my honesty and had become stronger in themselves through learning that I had the same problems as they had. Rather than my audiences getting smaller as people realize I'm no better than they are, they've become larger as people understand that if *I* can do it, despite my challenges, then so can *they*. And so can *you*!

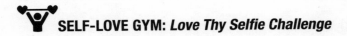 **SELF-LOVE GYM:** *Love Thy Selfie Challenge*

Earlier I suggested that you loved your selfie regardless of how you were feeling. So here's a vulnerability challenge. Take a few selfies of yourself throughout the week that show yourself not just at your best but also at your worst.

Let your selfies show how you really feel in both your happy moments and your sad ones.

Share them on social media using the hashtag #iheartmyselfie or simply #iheartme.

Open Up, Let Your Guard Down and Let the Magic In

The worst day of my life was when a specialist told us that Oscar, then only 22 months old, had bone cancer (osteosarcoma), that there was nothing we could do and that, at best, he had about six months to live. We could add three months to this by amputating his leg, but we'd need to weigh that up against the loss of quality of the remainder of his life.

It was unexpected. Life can throw curveballs from time to time. I won't go into too many details here. It all happened very recently. If you want to read more, I've placed a little update in the afterword.

The initial impact this had on us was traumatic. But this is also a story about allowing yourself to be vulnerable and the magic that you allow into your life when you do.

Elizabeth has always been a very private person. She's never let her guard down. Even when bullied at high school, she never let the bullies see her scared. Even when her parents learned of it and took her out of school a year early, she never let them see her real pain.

In all the years we've been together, I have never once known Elizabeth to tell anyone other than family and close friends anything significant about her life, about her real hopes, dreams, aspirations or especially her fears. Nor would she ever show emotion.

Oscar's diagnosis changed all that. In the days that followed, Elizabeth cried in front of people she hardly knew. She cried in front of our vets, Shelley, Stephanie and Helen, and the nurse, Louisa. She cried on the street when we told some neighbours and people who had dogs Oscar liked to play with. She cried in front of near strangers.

The magic was that Elizabeth allowed other people to care, and in so doing she created a little opening that invited them into her life for the first time ever. In the process she entered a little into theirs too. She allowed them to empathize and extend their compassion, sometimes with a caring face, sometimes with a gentle touch and other times just by sharing the space and allowing her to be how she needed to be right then. She allowed them to connect.

Vulnerability and compassion both invite relationships into a new space. They both break down any pretence. When we show compassion, we are being ourselves. When we feel someone's pain, we are being ourselves. When we show our own, we are being ourselves.

I had a similar experience to Elizabeth. When faced with sudden difficulty, I tend to get clarity and focus. In some ways this is very useful, because I tend to focus on a solution and move quickly to activate it. The downside is that I bottle up pain. Shifting my focus so quickly doesn't mean that the pain goes away. I just ignore it.

The day of the diagnosis, I went over to see my mum and dad. Like many families, we're not used to showing emotion in front of each other. Not since I was a child have I shown emotion in front of my dad. But that day, when Mum hugged me, I cried.

Coming out of the hug with my mum, I looked over at my dad. He quickly looked away. It wasn't a conscious decision, more a reflex reaction. He just didn't know what to say or do.

Usually, when I'm leaving to go back home, Mum comes to the door and gives me a goodbye hug. Dad usually just says goodbye from his chair. This time, he followed me to the door too.

The following week, at my niece's seventh birthday party, Dad came to the door as well. It was his way of being there for me and I understood it.

Simple though the gesture was, it brought a new depth and quality to my relationship with my dad. Expressing my pain added a new dimension to my relationship with my mum, too. I was giving her a chance to be my mum and pour out her compassion and I was able to witness a part of her I'd seen so often when I was a child.

Circumstances sometimes force us to be vulnerable. They ask us to step up, not to be stronger in the classical sense but to shake off all pretence and just stand there, naked. In those moments, it really doesn't matter what anyone thinks. But we give others permission to care. We invite them to be human. That's the magic in vulnerability.

Getting Some Leverage

Letting our guard down and being authentic is about the most important thing we can ever do. We just need to convince ourselves that the benefits far outweigh the risks.

OK, the risks:

♦ People might not like us.

♦ We might be distanced from a group.

♦ We might lose one or more of our relationships.

♦ People might say we've changed and get angry with us.

Let's do the benefits then:

♦ We let go of the stress of pretending we're something we're not.

♦ We can relax in our private moments without wondering how we're going to keep up the pretence or without resenting the people around us for expecting us to be something we're not.

♦ We might find that people show us a level of respect we've never known before.

♦ We know that people who leave our life weren't good for us anyway because they only liked the version of us that we'd been showing them.

♦ We make room in our life for people who love the real us, and we draw these people into our life.

♦ We form deeper, more authentic and meaningful relationships.

♦ We become healthier.

These are just some of the risks and benefits, ones that are fairly general. I'm certain that you can think of more in your own life, ones that relate more personally to you. That's why I'd like you to have a go at it yourself. It's an important exercise. Here's what to do.

SELF-LOVE GYM: *Being Authentic*

Consider these questions and write down your answers:

◆ What benefits would being more authentic bring you specifically? For example, which of your relationships would being authentic affect and how might they be affected? Would it affect your career?

◆ What actions could you take or conversations could you have in the next few days that would help you to be more authentic?

You can't be *enough* while you're hiding your true self, because the act of hiding affirms that you think you're *not* enough. Why else would you be hiding? Being authentic is about showing yourself as you really are. *Enough* says, 'I am here, now, as I am.'

At Your Own Pace

Being authentic means showing your vulnerabilities, but, as I mentioned earlier, that isn't about being a book that's open for everyone to see everything about you. It's about asking yourself if more authenticity or more vulnerability would be good for you and in which circumstances. It might only mean a small amount of opening up and letting your guard down or it might mean a lot. We're all different.

Personally, I'm learning to be more open and honest with more people. This has included sharing some personal examples in this book that I've not written about before. This was a little out of my comfort zone, but not too much. But I also have a small number of family and close friends with whom I share certain personal things that I wouldn't necessarily share with others. They're my inner circle, so to speak.

Self-love is about learning what works for you as an individual. There are times when vulnerability isn't the right thing. It can lead to being taken advantage of. That's always a risk, and one that we can't always avoid.

My friend Gillian reminded me of this. She told me that being vulnerable came naturally to her but she had to learn not to be such an open book. This was especially true during a time when she lost some members of her family. She was treated very poorly when she was at her most vulnerable and this was very isolating. Instead of acceptance and belonging, vulnerability led to loneliness for her.

Gillian learned that it was only safe to be vulnerable with certain people. This was a valuable lesson. The act of showing vulnerability in the presence of specific people shows we are *enough* far more than opening up to everyone. It becomes an empowered choice, and that shows we are in a state of *enough*.

In summary... Allowing ourselves to be vulnerable is a way to build the feeling that we are *enough*. Holding back is usually done out of fear of what people might think. But allowing that fear to call the shots only says, 'I am *not* enough.' Being vulnerable looks fear in the eye and says, 'I will not hide. Here I am, now, as I am.'

Vulnerability is part of being authentic. It's opening up to the world as we are. There's power in it. And greatness. It takes courage. It is a mark of courage because it always involves risk.

In your exploration of vulnerability, move at your own pace. Choose the people you let into your life and choose how far you open up to them. Owning those choices always says, 'I *am* enough.'

Chapter 9

The Law of Personal Gravity

'The privilege of a lifetime is to become who you really are.'

C. G. JUNG

Babies love themselves. They will never try to be anyone other than who they are. They don't know how. They are 100 per cent authentic. We are drawn to them, as if they have gravity.

Puppies love themselves too. They're also 100 per cent authentic. We're drawn to them too, as if they have gravity.

I call this 'the law of personal gravity'. It's the law that says:

'The more we are our authentic selves, the more people are drawn to us.'

As we grow up, though, as we get bigger and bigger, we actually get smaller and smaller. Our light diminishes. Our gravity weakens. It's because we cover our light with layer upon layer of ideas, notions and beliefs that convince us that we're *not* enough. For this reason, the gravity of a child is several times stronger than the gravity of most adults.

It's quite simple, really. Authenticity, vulnerability, honesty, courage, self-care – these all increase our gravity. Personal gravity is high when we know we're *enough* and weak when we believe we're *not* enough.

We can tell when someone feels they're *not* enough. Usually, we're not drawn to them as much as we are to other people. It's not that there's anything wrong with them. And it's not so much a conscious judgement. It's just that deep in our psyche, we all seek connection and we intuitively know if connection is possible with the people we meet.

It can even be that a person feels they're *not* enough, but they have a strong mind and a large personality which they use to draw people to them. But that's not gravity, it's overwhelming people. You can tell that it's not authentic.

Want to increase your gravity? Be your authentic self! And then you'll start to know that you *are* enough, and people will look at you and wonder what it is that makes you shine from the inside so much.

Increasing your personal gravity isn't about getting people to like you, though – although people liking you *is* a side effect. The goal is always to be your authentic self and therefore to come to know that you *are* enough.

Personal gravity is an indicator of authenticity, a barometer, if you will, of self-love. It operates whether we like it or not or whether we agree with it or not. But the more aware of it we are, the more we can use it to measure our progress.

We're not just playing a numbers game here. It's not necessarily that greater numbers of people are drawn to us when we have high personal gravity (although that often does happen), but that we attract greater depth and quality of connection.

So, if you find yourself consistently surrounded by people who make you feel uncomfortable, ask yourself why you have drawn them into your life. Is it a sign that you're not being as authentic as you could be? (Or is it your own authentic self that you're uncomfortable with? That would also indicate a self-love deficit.)

Personal gravity is also correlated with happiness and success in life. The more authentic we are, the more likely we are to feel good, and therefore the more productive, insightful and creative we become, and these things usually translate into success in whichever arena of life we place ourselves in.

People will also think we're lucky, but that too is a side effect of our gravity. Our gravity draws opportunities and events that aren't always obvious at first, but simmer in the background, growing in momentum until the time is right for them to enter our life.

So, before you go any further, write down your answer to the following question:

What can I do more of that says, 'This is who I really am!'?

The Law of Personal Repulsion

The law of personal gravity has an opposite, as most things do. It's called the law of personal repulsion. It's about how we repel people, success, hopes and dreams when we're not being ourselves.

Shortly after I resigned from the pharmaceutical industry I started reading self-help and spiritual books. I was inspired about starting out in my new career as a writer and speaker. Having read all those books, I somehow managed to get it into my head that I had to be enlightened to write and speak. So I decided to be enlightened.

Everywhere I went, I tried to show I was a peaceful and enlightened being. I regurgitated lines I'd read in books and passed them off as my own. Often, I even spoke in a gentle way because I thought it was how an enlightened person would speak.

My former university chemistry professor, William J. Kerr, likes to organize reunions with some of the students he has taught. In 2000, about six months after I'd left the pharmaceutical industry, I attended one such gathering.

My university days were some of the most enjoyable of my life. I had great friends, I studied hard, learned a lot, played a lot of sport and even found time to be president of the Chemistry Society. I had lots of energy and would get fairly enthusiastic and excitable when I was part of a group. I loved to tell stories and jokes and to laugh.

But that was over. Now that I was enlightened, I couldn't behave in that kind of way. It was so unevolved.

So, at the reunion weekend I walked everywhere slowly, usually with my hands clasped behind my back. I'd seen some monks do that and figured I should be doing it too. I also wore a serene smile on my face, and when I spoke, it was softly and gently. I wanted people to know that I was enlightened. It would inspire them.

On the first night after dinner there were about 25 of us in a large lounge talking, telling stories and having a laugh – or at least everyone else was. At university, when someone told a story, I'd usually chip in with a similar one, and I might even have embellished it a little at times, just to make it funnier. So now, as each story ended, my friends instinctively looked at me to top it. But I just sat there, cross-legged, with a serene smile on my face, nodding pleasantly.

Unsurprisingly, my career as a writer and speaker didn't exactly take off. I wasn't attracting audiences to my speaking events because all I was doing was regurgitating what other people had said and trying to pretend that I was enlightened. Had I been myself, a guy who had a dream and had left his job to pursue it, or maybe if I'd even just talked about some of the lessons *I'd* learned in life, I might have been more successful during that period. But success follows authenticity. People can tell where you're at and I wasn't being authentic. I had negative gravity. I was repelling what I wanted in my life. It wasn't long before I was financially broke.

Much later I realized there's nothing wrong with having a laugh or being the centre of attention if that's the sort of person you are. I used to think that being spiritual meant being at peace. But the truest spirituality is being who you really are.

Being at peace is part of that. But it doesn't mean having no thoughts whatsoever. It means being at peace with who you are. It means accepting yourself – your imperfections, your flaws, your wobbly bits, your vulnerabilities, your habits, the fact that you get scared, the fact that you don't know what to do a lot of the time, the fact you're not always confident, the fact that sometimes you feel like a complete mess, as well as all the positive things about yourself. Being at peace with all that boosts your gravity.

All of us have 'stuff', baggage, regrets. We get the idea that we need to eliminate all that to be healed. That's not true at all. Peace is when we *accept* it all. And if we can be at peace with ourselves, we'll be *enough*.

Life Goes On...

Accepting ourselves needn't mean that we no longer grow, or pursue our hopes and dreams. Growth, like change, is natural and healthy when it originates from a sense of *enough*. It's perfectly natural to sense possibilities for expansion and improvement and to follow them up.

Equally, when we accept ourselves, life doesn't cease to be challenging. We don't sit on a metaphorical white cloud in a state of perpetual peace. We simply meet people, challenges and experiences with a healthier mindset. Life goes on, pretty much as usual.

As it goes on, we can learn a lot from watching animals. Oscar knows who he is. He chases ducks and other birds when we're at the river. If he goes too close to swans, they ward him off with a guttural 'kchh' sound. And I'm fairly confident he doesn't think, *That swan is hissing at me. Maybe it doesn't like me. I wonder if I've done something to offend it.* He just gets on with sniffing trees and dog wee.

Oscar has taught me lots. One big lesson is that my gravity diminishes when I'm overly obsessed with what people think of me and whether they like me or not.

I believe Oscar and I were always meant to find each other. In fact he has helped me to find myself.

I bet you have an animal or a person in your life right now who is teaching you about yourself. Pause for a moment and think about it! Who is teaching you who you are? Who is bringing out your authentic self? Or who is *forcing* you to see your authentic self?

The following exercise is about discovering what makes you who you are. When you know that, you'll find it easier to be authentic.

And when you find your real self, the people who need to be in your life will find you, too.

SELF-LOVE GYM: *Who Are You?*

Take some time to reflect on everything that makes you uniquely *you*. Think about the good stuff, but include your wobbly bits too. And your hopes and dreams, because they are part of you. Even include how you act when you fail, because that's part of you too.

Think about the people who have influenced you, helped mould your character, helped you be who you are, provided the environment in which you became yourself...

Think about the events that have influenced you – those that have helped you display your character, those that have forged your character...

Draw or paint who you are, or write it all down as a poem if you prefer.

In summary... Authenticity creates gravity. Just as apples fall from trees due to the Earth's gravity, people fall towards us due to our personal gravity.

This law of personal gravity, as I like to call it, also has an opposite: the law of personal repulsion. We harness that law when we're not being authentic.

Children and puppies have a lot of personal gravity. Adults tend to have much less, mostly because on the way to adulthood we've learned to think of ourselves as *not* enough. But as we learn that we are, indeed, and always have been, *enough*, our gravity increases again.

The goal isn't to have gravity, of course. The goal is to be authentic and to know we're *enough*. Gravity is just an observable indicator of our progress.

Part III

You
Matter

'Life is short, break the rules. Forgive
quickly, kiss slowly. Love truly. Laugh
uncontrollably and never regret
anything that makes you smile.'

MARK TWAIN

Chapter 10

Self-Compassion

*'Never forget that once upon a
time, in an unguarded moment, you
recognized yourself as a friend.'*

ELIZABETH GILBERT, *EAT, PRAY, LOVE*

It was the middle of the night when Dobby the house elf appeared in Harry Potter's bedroom at 4 Privet Drive to tell Harry that he was in mortal danger.

Passing that information to Harry, however, was forbidden. It was a betrayal of the Malfoys, Dobby's masters. So each time he gave Harry some information, he inflicted pain upon himself. Initially he bashed his head against a window. In later scenes in the book, he struck himself with objects instead.

While few of us bash our heads on windows or hit ourselves with objects when we do something wrong, we do the same kind of thing with words. A lady who attended one of my workshops said that if she called other people by the names she called herself a lot of the time, she'd have a criminal record by now.

If self-criticism were an Olympic sport, it would be very difficult to win a medal. So many people are so good at it that there'd be a huge number contesting the medals.

When I was a child, when someone called you names you'd chant: 'Sticks and stones may break my bones, but names will never hurt me.' Useful as the saying was in terms of defiance, it was merely an irritant to the person doing the name-calling and did nothing at all to diffuse the pain of being attacked with poisonous words.

The truth is, words hurt. We all know that. Not only do they hurt when someone else uses them against us, they hurt just as much when we use them against ourselves. And the problem is, we do the latter much, much, much more often. Do any of the following sound familiar?

◆ 'I'm such an idiot!'

◆ 'I can't believe I said/did that.'

◆ 'I'm such a failure.'

◆ 'I'm a screw-up.'

◆ 'I'm just no good at that.'

◆ 'I'm never going to be any good at that.'

◆ 'I'm so fat and ugly.'

◆ 'I'm disgusted with myself.'

Not pleasant, is it? Who wants to listen to that?

An Antidote to Self-Criticism

Would you criticize a child for falling on their first attempts to walk? Would you brand them a failure? I don't think you would. I'll hazard a guess that you allow everyone else to be a child, stumbling, falling and feeling their way through life as they learn to walk and then run, but criticize yourself for not being able to run on the first attempt.

But we're all like children. We all stumble and fall through life. We all screw up. We all make mistakes. We're only human.

Self-compassion acknowledges all this and softly says, 'It's OK.'

Self-compassion is an antidote to self-criticism. It's having compassion for yourself. It's taking action to relieve pain or disappointment, sometimes with a few kind thoughts or words for yourself, sometimes with a hot bath and sometimes even with a tub of ice-cream. Self-compassion is soft, in contrast to the hardness of self-criticism.

If Dobby had showed some self-compassion, he might have said something like: 'Harry Potter, I'm not supposed to share my masters' secrets. I am a house elf and it is forbidden to betray my masters. But I believe I'm doing the right thing. You are in danger and I want to help you. So, even though I've done something technically wrong, I know my heart is in the right place and I'm not going to be hard on myself.'

Of course, Dobby wasn't very self-compassionate. He hit his head against the window instead.

A Buffer When Things Go Wrong

I remember when my book *Why Kindness is Good for You* was published I was very proud of it because I'd spent many months collating all the evidence I could find that showed that kindness and compassion were healthy. I'd also included one or two inspirational stories of kindness. My goal with the book was to inspire more people to be kind. I've always believed that kindness can change the world. Now I was getting lots of national newspaper and magazine publicity and radio interviews and was due to appear on a breakfast TV show. I was on a high.

Yet a day after the book was released, the very first review posted on Amazon UK was a one-star review. It was from a gentleman who I presume hadn't actually read the whole book and had completely misinterpreted it. He said that I encouraged people to be kind purely to make themselves feel good. I wasn't entirely sure how he got that from the book. I could only conclude that he'd read the title and the back cover then skimmed through a few pages to find 'evidence' to back up his belief.

But I was shattered. My face flushed when I read the review. All that work and now no one would buy the book.

Over the next few days, as more and more people purchased and read the book, I was relieved to find it started racking up five-star reviews. I felt much better as they began appearing.

The experience taught me two valuable things, though. First, I realized that my feelings of worth were wrapped up in how the book was received. And second, I didn't have self-compassion.

It wasn't so much that I was a self-critic, but I had no soft place to land when things went badly. Self-compassion is that soft place. It's the part of us that softly squeezes our own shoulder and tells us, kindly, that everything is going to be alright, it's not the end of the world and that whatever happens, we're still here.

Self-compassion buffers the pain of disappointment. It stops us from taking everything so personally. It reminds us that it's OK to have a bad day, it's OK to fail, and that we haven't failed anyway just because we don't feel happy, or we haven't been successful, or we're not in a relationship, or we're broke. There's always tomorrow.

Self-compassion highlights an important difference between self-love and self-esteem. Most of the time those terms can be used interchangeably, and I've done so throughout this book. But sometimes, people get their self-esteem from their successes and achievements. Then, when things go wrong, they suffer badly. Their self-esteem is like a boat on the ocean, rising and falling with every wave.

Self-love is wider than self-esteem. It contains self-compassion, whereas self-esteem does not. When we have true self-love, when disappointment comes, we understand that it's OK. These things happen. We know *we* aren't a failure, it's just that something hasn't turned out quite right. We understand that we need support, kindness and compassion and that we're entitled to it. So we offer ourselves support and kindness, or even seek some extra in the arms of a loved one or friend, but we're doing so because we know that we deserve it. We *are* enough.

With self-compassion, disappointment is not nearly so painful. Self-compassion also helps us to extract our worth from our successes and achievements, reinforcing that we *are* enough. And when we're striving for a goal, it stops us judging ourselves as *not* enough right up until we achieve that goal.

All this and it's healthy too!

Self-Compassion is Healthy
'Make Mine a Triple'

From research into self-compassion, it's now clear that it is a triple anti-inflammatory.[1] This means it reduces three kinds of inflammation:

1. biological inflammation

2. inflammation towards the self (self-criticism)

3. inflammation in relationships

a) Self-compassion reduces biological inflammation

A 2014 study checked out the connection between self-compassion and stress-induced inflammation. That sounded like a mouthful, didn't it?

Before we go any further, I want to point out that inflammation isn't necessarily a bad guy. It's actually a vital part of the immune response to injury. It's most obvious in the redness and swelling that occurs around the site of a wound. This helps draw blood, oxygen and repair nutrients to the wound site, aiding the healing process.

It occurs on the inside of the body too, as the body tends to the 'wounds' of stress and unhealthy lifestyle choices. Again, it's simply doing its job of helping the body return to health. The problem arises when there's too much inflammation occurring too much of the time, which is a symptom of consistent stress and unhealthy living. In time, if we lack a way of dealing with our daily stressors, frustrations and annoyances, stress-induced inflammation mounts up and can cause all kinds of collateral damage in the body, including cardiovascular disease, and even increase the risk of cancer.

Inflammation like this can be thought of like a tap dripping water into a sink with a plug in it. Eventually the sink fills up and spills over, causing collateral damage to the floor.

To measure self-compassion in the study, participants responded with 'I agree' or 'I disagree' to a series of statements. Responding with 'I agree' to a statement like 'I try to be understanding and patient toward aspects of my personality I do not like' would indicate self-compassion. Responding with 'I disagree' would show a lack of self-compassion in that area. Responding with 'I disagree' to a statement like 'I am disapproving of and judgemental about my own flaws and inadequacies' would indicate self-compassion. Responding with 'I agree' would indicate self-criticism.

The study, which involved 41 volunteers, found that those who had more self-compassion had a lower level of stress-induced inflammation. Their bloodstreams were clearer of inflammation.[2]

Think about what that means! Self-compassion protects biology. As well as being protective against stress-induced inflammation, it is now understood to be protective against the diseases linked to it, and these include cardiovascular disease, cancer, arthritis, diabetes and even Alzheimer's disease.

Think of it as akin to putting a high-quality rubber seal on the tap so it stops dripping and at the same time pulling the plug out of the sink.

In a 2009 study, researchers actually taught people self-compassion as part of a compassion programme to study the effects of compassion (for self and others) on inflammation.[3] They enrolled 33 people between the ages of 17 and 19 into a six-week training programme, part of which involved learning strategies for being more self-compassionate and practising the loving-kindness meditation. This is a Buddhist meditation which we'll look at more closely later. The volunteers were compared to 28 people in the same age group who didn't learn self-compassion, but who attended health group discussions for the same time periods instead. This was the control group.

After the six-week period was over, the volunteers were all given a task that was designed to stress them so that the scientists could measure stress-induced inflammation. The task is known as a TSST (Trier Social Stressor Test). The people who had learned self-compassion had much lower levels of inflammation than those in the control group. The amount of practice also mattered. Those who did the most sessions per week (six to nine) had much lower levels of inflammation than those who did the fewest (one or two sessions).

b) Self-compassion reduces self-inflammation (self-criticism)

The second type of inflammation countered by self-compassion is self-inflammation, which is what self-criticism is.

The loving-kindness meditation has been shown to substantially reduce self-criticism, especially in people who are very good at it … the self-criticism, that is.

In a 2014 study, 38 volunteers who scored highly on an assessment of self-criticism were randomized to either practise the loving-kindness meditation or be part of a control group. There were 19 in each group.

The study found that the volunteers who had learned self-compassion were significantly less self-critical than they had been at the start. And a three-month follow-up that was designed to see if the effects would last showed that the meditation group had maintained the reduction in self-criticism. They had not gone back to their old self-critical ways. They had learned a new, gentler, way of treating themselves.[4]

Another study involving 139 people found that a seven-week course in loving-kindness meditation increased daily experiences of positive emotions, including love, joy, gratitude, contentment, hope, pride, interest, amusement and awe.

These emotional gains impacted the participants in multiple ways. They felt a greater sense of purpose. They had more mastery over their lives. They also felt greater life satisfaction. They felt more optimistic about the future. They enjoyed improvements in the quality of their relationships. Oh, and their overall health improved too.[5]

c) Self-compassion reduces relationship inflammation

The loving-kindness meditation helps reduce the inflammation of difficult relationships. It's especially powerful in helping to improve personal relationships that are in trouble, whether those are with loved ones, work colleagues or even people who are seen as enemies. During the meditation, we cultivate a sense of love and compassion towards the person (or people) who are challenging us. When we do this, feelings of hostility are gradually replaced by gentleness.

Some of us, of course, *want* to remain hostile towards certain people. Some people hold on to anger for years. They think those involved deserve it. They may do. But hostility towards others is extremely unhealthy for *us*. Do we deserve *that*?

In fact, if our goal is to develop cardiovascular disease, hostility towards others is one of the fastest ways to get it. It's at least as efficient as having an unhealthy diet. Consistent hostility and aggression in relationships is strongly linked with hardening of the arteries. In a piece of startling symmetry, where the outside reflects the inside, scientists found that as we harden towards others, we harden on the inside too. The research has been called 'Hard Marriage, Hard Heart'.[6]

It was the outcome of a study of married couples. Their behaviour and ways of communicating with each other were noted and each couple was scored according to whether they showed love, kindness, compassion, patience and affection or whether they showed hostility and aggression and were domineering or bullying.

The results were very clear. Those who were most hostile had the highest levels of coronary artery calcification, or CAC for short. It's where the coronary artery moves from having the internal consistency of a lightly poached egg to something resembling plasterboard.

The arterial damage was not caused by diet or lifestyle. It was caused by hostility and aggression.

Self-compassion is a powerful antidote to hostility, aggression and anger. The loving-kindness meditation is especially effective, because as well as cultivating compassion for ourselves, it cultivates empathy and compassion for others.

As we soften on the inside (emotionally and also biologically), we begin to soften on the outside, in our interactions with people, and this softens relationships. It also helps foster a sense of trust and connection with people we don't know very well, even total strangers. It helps build social connectedness.

This was the finding of a Stanford University study where 45 volunteers practised the loving-kindness meditation even just briefly for a few minutes a day. They were compared with 48 volunteers in a control group who didn't do the meditation.[7]

The version of the meditation was simple. Each person would imagine two loved ones standing on either side of them and they would send their love to them. Some people imagined sending love as a pink ball of light, others just wished them love, health and happiness, others used words. Any way proved as good as any other. Then they would imagine sending those loving, compassionate feelings to a neutral stranger.

Even a brief meditation practice helped the volunteers to feel more connected to loved ones *and* complete strangers.

When it comes to getting on in the world, forming relationships is key. And the key to forming relationships is letting our barriers down and allowing connections to happen. As you know, that occurs through having courage to be ourselves and not hide our vulnerabilities. It also occurs through self-compassion.

With practice, the loving-kindness meditation helps build trust and compassion at an automatic level. In other words, we don't even have to think about it.

Compassion and the Vagus Nerve

The star of the show in how compassion, whether for ourselves or another person, reduces inflammation is the vagus nerve. This nerve is the longest cranial nerve in the body, stretching from the top of the brain stem throughout the body. It gets its name from the medieval Latin for 'wandering', as it is so long it pretty much wanders all through the body, interfacing with the heart, the stomach and other organs.

Compassion and the vagus nerve work closely together. Scientists say they are 'correlated', in that a person who is very compassionate usually has high vagal tone (akin to muscle tone). High vagal tone is healthy because it means that even when we give the vagus nerve a lot of work to do, it can still keep inflammation low, just as a person who is physically fit can handle more physical exertion than people who are not in such good condition.

The vagus nerve is the body's number one way of controlling inflammation. Following injury, inflammation rises to the optimum required for healing. Once at that level, the vagus nerve puts the brakes on it and ensures it doesn't get out of hand. It keeps inflammation at bay on the inside of the body as well. It works through sending a signal into the immune cells and right through to the DNA. The signal tells certain inflammatory genes to switch off.

In a real way, then, the effects of self-compassion run throughout the nervous system right to the genetic level. How amazing is that?

Given that one of the major pain-management strategies in the world is the use of anti-inflammatory drugs, it also explains why research shows that practising the loving-kindness meditation can reduce pain in chronic pain sufferers. When inflammation is turned down at the genetic level, pain lessens.

In one study, 43 chronic back-pain volunteers either participated in an eight-week course in the loving-kindness meditation or received standard care for their back pain. At the end of the study, the volunteers who did the meditation had significantly less pain.[8]

Also concerning back pain, a study conducted at Boston College showed that patients suffering from chronic back pain benefited from helping other pain sufferers. It was called 'patient to peer' and the intensity of pain significantly dropped in the sufferers who helped other sufferers.[9]

Wouldn't you like to learn some strategies for developing self-compassion?

Self-Compassion Strategy 1: Swap a Thought

One of the ways we can learn self-compassion is through training ourselves to think differently. Inner harshness is a habit. And, just like any habit, it can be changed with a bit of practice. And I say 'practice' because, like anything, to get good at something we need to practise it. No one ever became an Olympic medalist after going out for a jog just the once!

If we practise self-compassion, we'll get good at self-compassion. So let's get started.

SELF-LOVE GYM: *Swap a Thought*

One of the simplest strategies for developing self-compassion is to swap a self-defeating thought for a gentle one. This exercise is about making a stock of gentle thoughts to draw from.

♦   Make a list of some of the ways you've shown kindness or compassion to someone, or when you've shown patience or gentleness.

♦   Make a list of your positive attributes, your skills and your achievements.

♦   Make a third list, this time of instances when you've coped with a difficult challenge or when you've shown courage.

♦   And make a fourth list of some of your happiest memories.

♦   Now, each time you catch yourself in the act of self-criticism, take a deep breath in, release it gently, then recite or visualize one or more of the items from your lists.

It may sound simplistic, but two things happen when you do this. The first is that the intake of breath moves your attention away from the criticism. While this happens, it drives brain resources away from the stress centres of the brain and towards more conscious control areas. It prevents you from getting involved in a train of self-abusive thinking.

The second thing that happens is that by substituting the self-critical thought for a positive memory you lessen the impact of the inner harshness.

The skill is in being able to catch yourself in the throes of being harsh on yourself and substituting those thoughts for one or more of the items from your lists. But, as I said, you will improve with practice.

It may seem unlikely that just recalling some positive things about yourself can ease self-criticism, but it does. If you're really good at self-criticism, you got there through practice too. You're basically just learning to change what you're practising.

After some time, you will rewire your brain networks. If normal for you has been self-criticism, normal will become patience, understanding and self-compassion instead.

I've explained the neuroscience of this for a reason. I've learned that when you know what's happening in the brain, you're more likely to actually do the work!

Self-Compassion Strategy 2: Do the Loving-Kindness Meditation

The loving-kindness meditation is a powerful tool for developing self-compassion. Also known as *metta*, it is traditionally a Buddhist meditation. You might be familiar with it. Many people are. Most think of it as all about compassion towards others, which is a big part of its purpose, but the first line in the meditation is for the self:

'May I be filled with loving-kindness. May I be well, peaceful and at ease, happy and free of suffering.'

The focus of the loving-kindness meditation is to build a sentiment of compassion and kindness for ourselves, our loved ones, people who are neutral to us, difficult people in our life and everyone in the world. Each time, our circle of compassion widens.

SELF-LOVE GYM: *Do the Loving-Kindness Meditation*

There are five sayings in the loving-kindness meditation.

♦ It starts with yourself. You say, three times,

'May I be filled with loving-kindness. May I be well, peaceful and at ease, happy and free of suffering.'

Sometimes it's useful to place your hand gently on your heart area as you say the words.

I've personally found that repeating simply 'I am filled ... etc.' works well for developing self-compassion. There's no definite rule that says you need to use 'May I'. Just do the version that feels better for you. Have a play around with both versions and see which suits you better.

♦ Next you build the sentiment towards a loved one, repeating, again three times:

'May [name of the person] be filled with loving-kindness. May he/she be well, peaceful and at ease, happy and free of suffering.'

If you're a visually oriented person you'll find it useful to picture the person at this point, and so on throughout the meditation.

♦ Then you do the same three repetitions for a neutral person. That's someone you see around but don't really know. Maybe you pass them in the corridor at work. Maybe it's a person who scans your shopping at the supermarket.

♦ Then it's a difficult person. This might even be a loved one. Some people use the same person as their loved one and their difficult person. Some people use a person that they have a challenge with, maybe from work, or someone they've been in conflict with in the past. Some people use bullies, either from the present or the past.

♦ Finally, you project the sentiment out into the world, repeating three times:

'May all sentient beings be filled with loving-kindness. May they be well, peaceful and at ease, happy and free of suffering.'

This completes one cycle.

You can do as many or as few cycles as you wish. If you want to do more, you start again with yourself. You can then focus on a different loved one or the same person, a different neutral person or the same one and a different difficult person or the same one before completing the cycle with all sentient beings. Some people like to do several cycles, working through all of their closest loved ones but focusing each cycle on the same difficult person.

There's no specific rule that says you have to do the meditation in a particular way. It's all about the sentiment, so whatever you need to do to build the sentiment is fine. You don't even need to do it in the way I've described. Some people follow a protocol like the one in the study above, where they visualize two loved ones and two strangers. Some people even add 'Dear Lord' as in 'Dear Lord, May [person] be filled with loving-kindness ... [etc.]' It becomes, for them, the loving-kindness prayer rather than the loving-kindness meditation.

Self-Compassion Strategy 3: Listen to Your Inner Buddha

Dobby might not know it, but he has an inner Buddha. That's a wise, compassionate part of himself that is very far removed from the part of himself that uses objects for self-flagellation. When Dobby is punishing himself, the dominant voice inside his head is his self-critic. But there's also a part of Dobby who feels criticized. All in all, that's three parts: the critic, the criticized and the Buddha.

It's the same for all of us. When we give ourselves a harsh time, the main voice we listen to is that of our inner critic. So a very useful self-compassion strategy is to listen to our inner Buddha instead. It's all about shifting our attention.

♦ **SELF-LOVE GYM:** *Listen to Your Inner Buddha*

♦ Take a piece of paper and three pens, in different colours, one for the critic, one for the criticized and one for the inner Buddha.

The *critic* is your voice of self-criticism. It might sound like the voice or words of a parent, a sibling, a schoolteacher or even a husband or wife.

The *criticized* is the part of you who feels hurt through being criticized.

The *inner Buddha* is your wisest, most compassionate self.

♦ Choose something you normally give yourself a hard time about. Take up a pen and write down what the critic has to say about it. Write the words as you usually hear them. You can write harsh words in capital letters if that makes them feel more real for you.

♦ Then pick up a different-coloured pen and write as the criticized. Say how you feel about being criticized. Does it hurt? Then say that! You might explain what you're trying to do and say that criticism doesn't help at all, in fact it only holds you back. Say anything you want to say. Be truthful.

Allow the critic to respond if you feel it needs to respond.

You can switch back and forth as many times as you like between the critic and the criticized, just as you would in a conversation between two people. There's no hurry to complete the exercise in seven minutes or something! If it takes three hours, then it takes three hours.

♦ Whenever you feel the time is right, pick up a third coloured pen and allow your inner Buddha to have a say. As the kindest, gentlest, most loving and compassionate aspect of your soul, what would it say? How would it say it? Would it address you? The critic? Both?

When the inner Buddha has spoken, allow either the critic or criticized to respond if necessary. Again, you can go on and on in a dialogue for as long as you like. Continue until you feel that everything has been said. Make sure, though, that the inner Buddha gets the last word.

When the dialogue is complete, an addition to the exercise, if you want to do it, is to write a letter to yourself from your inner Buddha. It can be as long or as short as you wish. Then post the letter. That will allow you to be reminded of the wisdom in a day or two, when the letter arrives in the post.

Self-Compassion Strategy 4: Strike a Compassion Pose

Remember the power pose from earlier? Power posing shows that thoughts, feelings, brain chemistry and behaviour are all affected by what we do with our body. More broadly speaking, *any* body posture does the same. So why not strike a compassion pose?

SELF-LOVE GYM: *Strike a Compassion Pose*

I've found that if you strike a compassion pose, you can tilt your thoughts, feelings, brain chemistry and behaviour towards self-compassion. You can also extend your pose to a compassion-for-others pose.

◆ So, either sitting or standing, assume a posture or go through a set of movements that show self-compassion. You might, for instance, relax your facial muscles, soften your eyes and break into a soft, kind smile. (You can practise this in front of a mirror if you find it easier.) You might find you want to place your hands on your heart, give yourself a little squeeze or even a hug.

◆ Hold the pose for two minutes, just as you would a power pose.

Practising this regularly is an excellent way of using this powerful trick of neuroscience to train yourself to feel compassion for yourself and compassion for others.

In summary... Self-compassion is an antidote to self-criticism and also a buffer from pain when things don't go to plan. It's the art of treating ourselves with the same patience, understanding and kindness that we would extend to others when we make a mistake, feel hurt or disappointed, or fail at something.

It's extremely healthy, countering inflammation inside the body and therefore offering protection from disease. It's actually a triple anti-inflammatory in that it reduces not only biological inflammation but also self-inflammation (self-criticism) and relationship inflammation.

To learn self-compassion we can use strategies such as swapping a thought, doing the loving-kindness meditation, listening to our inner Buddha and striking a compassion pose.

Chapter 11

Forgiveness

'One of the keys to happiness is a bad memory.'
RITA MAE BROWN

All of us have made mistakes. All of us have made errors of judgement. All of us have hurt another person. At one time or another, all of us have behaved less than admirably, sometimes with painful consequences. One thing we all need is forgiveness.

Forgiving Ourselves

One of the stumbling blocks that gets in the way of self-love or self-compassion for some people is not being able to forgive themselves. 'How can I love myself when I did *that*?' is a common sentiment.

This is where self-forgiveness comes in. You're not alone if you have regrets. Everyone has them. Some people have major regrets and some people have minor ones. But the important thing to know is that *everyone* has them.

For our own health and sanity, it's important to be able to move past these blocks. For a start, forgiveness, like self-compassion, is extremely healthy. Research has shown that forgiveness, either of ourselves or others, is good for the heart.[1] It actually widens our arteries and increases blood flow to the heart. It also reduces blood pressure and heart rate. It improves coronary function in people who have had a heart attack. It improves the immune system. People who learn to forgive are less likely to feel depressed, angry, resentful, hurt, stressed, anxious or have a need for revenge. On the whole, forgiveness is a very healthy thing indeed.

Try the following self-forgiveness process on for size.

SELF-LOVE GYM: *Self-Forgiveness*

♦ Reflect on some of the ways in which forgiveness is good for your health (listed above). Some people find it useful to draw this as a picture. For example, you might draw your heart with a smiley face on it or a picture of yourself looking relaxed and at peace.

♦ Is judging yourself for past mistakes doing you any good? If not, why not? For example, is it affecting your health – mental or physical? Think about this. Is it holding you back in your life?

♦ How could your life be better if you let go of thinking about yourself in this way?

♦ Write a positive statement or an affirmation that will help you whenever the old way of thinking pops into your mind again. You might use something like 'I choose to let this go and in doing so I set myself free.'

♦ Now work on some self-compassion. Reflect on how everyone makes mistakes, makes errors of judgement, hurts people, loses sight of themselves from time to time... Reflect on the fact that we're only human.

♦ Now consider what your inner Buddha would say to you about this issue. If you were helping a loved one to forgive and they had this issue, what would you say to them and how would you say it?

♦ Atonement. This isn't always necessary, but do it if it feels important to you. If you have hurt or offended someone in the past, is there a way that you can make amends now? Could you apologize? Or could you act in some other way to balance things out? For instance, if you once hurt an ex-partner by having an affair, could you make a donation to a charity that supports people in distress?

The self-forgiveness process can be done as often as you feel it's necessary until the issue is sufficiently resolved. Many people like to do it weekly on the same issue for four to six weeks. Others like to do it daily over four consecutive days. The thing with forgiveness is that it's a process that shouldn't be rushed. It's not about looking for that magic bullet, that single thought that releases all pain from the past. OK, that sometimes happens, but for most people, most of the time, revisiting an issue repetitively is the most powerful way of finding some peace.

Here's another, very simple, self-forgiveness process:

🏋 SELF-LOVE GYM: *'What Was My Intention?'*

Let's say you hurt someone's feelings once and you regret it. Say it was a spouse, family member or close friend (these are the most common).

♦ Did you really mean to hurt the person or were you just overwhelmed or confused? Ask yourself, 'What was my intention?' Get past the surface stuff of what you were thinking at the time, even if you were angry and wanted to hurt the person.

- Imagine standing there as an observer and looking at your own face. Does your face look angry? What's underneath the anger? Hurt, perhaps? Pain?

- Look even closer. What's underneath that? Fear? Fear of not being loved? Fear of loss of connection or belonging?

- Ask yourself again, 'What was my intention? Did I want to hurt the other person or did I want them to understand my pain or my fear?'

No one *really* wants to hurt someone else (with a few exceptions). That's why we feel so bad afterwards, why we feel regret. It's actually our love for a person that often causes us to lash out. Perhaps we love someone but fear they will stop loving us back.

How many times have you uttered the words 'I didn't mean to hurt you'? And I bet you really didn't. So this is a useful exercise in self-compassion and self-forgiveness because it helps to remind you that it's usually fear that motivates hurtful words or behaviour, and underneath the fear lies love.

This doesn't change what happened, but it allows you to be a little more sensitive towards your own pain of regret.

Forgiving Others

Forgiving others is a natural side effect of self-love. It's also why some people resist self-love work: 'I don't want to start feeling compassion for people who deserve what they get. I'm not letting them off the hook!'

Forgiveness isn't about saying that someone's behaviour was acceptable. It's simply a choice to let go of the past so that we can move on with our future.

Holding on to anger about someone else is also quite unhealthy and the benefits of forgiveness are many, especially for the heart and emotions.

. . . .

♥ SELF-LOVE GYM: *A Process for Forgiving Others*

Here's the process for forgiving others. You'll notice that it's very similar to the self-forgiveness process.

◆ Reflect on how and why forgiveness is good for your health.

◆ Ask yourself if it's doing you any good to hold on to the past. If not, why not? What have been some of the consequences of holding on to a past hurt or grievance?

◆ Write down how forgiveness will positively affect your future.

◆ Write down a positive statement or an affirmation to say to yourself the next time a thought about the issue comes up. You might use something like, '*I choose to let this go and in doing so I set myself free.*'

◆ Many people tell others about their past, especially when they meet new people. If this is you, and your past is full of old grievances, write down a different way of talking about your past that reflects your intent to move ahead positively. Then you will have it ready the next time you meet someone new.

◆ Build empathy. Reflect on the fact that you've also hurt people in the past. Remind yourself that we're all human. Find a little understanding of the person who hurt you, no matter how difficult that may be. This isn't about letting them off scot-free. It's just so that you can find a little more peace in yourself.

◆ Write down some of the benefits of what happened to you. For instance, if your partner had an affair in the past, you might reflect on the fact that you have a new partner, children and great friends that you might never have had if you'd stayed with that person.

The purpose of this step is to change your perception of the past.

Like the self-forgiveness process, this is also a process that shouldn't be rushed. You can do it daily or weekly until you feel the issue has been resolved to a sufficient degree.

In summary... With both self-forgiveness and forgiveness of others we can get to a place where we can see the benefit of forgiveness in our life. We may even go further and come to understand, for instance, that there is nothing to forgive, that everything happens as it's meant to. Or that everything and everyone is an expression of love, or God, and that mistakes are simply growth. We might even find comfort in the idea that souls agree to hurt or offend each other so that we can all grow through the experience.

However we view it, what's important here is that forgiveness, whether of ourselves or another person, dissolves blocks to growth and in so doing paves the way to self-love.

Chapter 12

What Are You Doing for Yourself?

'What determines the level of self-esteem is what the individual does.'

Nathaniel Branden, *The Six Pillars of Self-Esteem*

It's an important question! Seriously, what are you doing for yourself?

Given you're reading this book, I'll take a guess at not very much. Don't worry; you're not alone.

Maybe you've gone so long without doing anything for yourself, while giving a lot of your time, love, care and attention to others, that if I were to ask you, 'What do you want?' or 'What do you need?', you'd think for a second and say, 'Nothing, really.' But I'll bet that it's not that you actually *don't* want or need anything. It's just that you've gone so long not doing anything for yourself that it's become quite difficult, alien even, to think of what you *do* want. This is a common symptom of 'I'm *not* enough.'

But is it really true that you couldn't do with some time for yourself? Is it really true that you wouldn't like to organize your life more, or focus a bit more on pursuing a hope or a dream, or reading books that you've forgotten you enjoy? Or even making space in your life for a relationship if you're single or adding more zing to a relationship if you're attached?

Would you like to have more meaning in your life? Would you like to have a sense of purpose that makes you excited about getting out of bed in the morning because you can't wait to start your day? Would you like to have mastery over your finances instead of having too much month left at the end of your money? Would you like to be physically fitter or to improve your diet?

It's hard to think these things when you're in *not* enough because it doesn't seem possible. Normal is being there for everyone else. It's like a well-worn path. Believe me, I know what that feels like. I'm writing these words from experience. I was that person who always responded with, 'Nothing, really.' I actually took pride in not wanting anything. I convinced myself it was an enlightened thing. The truth is, I just wasn't used to focusing on what I needed, so I no longer knew what I needed. I'd forged an identity as the person who was always kind. I attached my self-worth to that identity. The trouble was, I'd forgotten that I also needed to be kind to myself.

What Do You Want? What Do You Need?

So, why not start being kind to yourself right now? There's no better time than the present.

SELF-LOVE GYM: *Your Wants and Needs*

Here are the questions again:

♦ 'What do you want?'

♦ 'What do you need?'

♦ Or, if you struggle with that, try it this way around: 'What are you neglecting? What's missing in your life?'

Please don't read any further. Pick up a pen. Get some paper. If there isn't any available right now, find a blank page at the back of this book and write on that. Yes, think about what you want and need and write it down. Now. Tap it into your phone as a text message, write it on a notes app on a Smartphone or tablet. Scratch it into the dirt below your feet if you have to, but write something, anything.

Even writing one thing is a step in the right direction. And you have 10 seconds, starting from... No – that was a joke! There's no time limit. I don't care if it takes you a month. Just start now.

OK, welcome back to the book. Have you listed your wants and needs?

The next step is to pick some of the ones that are really important to you and decide what you're going to do about them.

. . . .

SELF-LOVE GYM: *Your Wants and Needs... continued*

♦ Write down at least one action step you could take for each of the wants and needs on your list.

 For example, if you want to be healthier, you might decide to write yourself a diet plan or get advice on one. Or perhaps you've been neglecting a dream of being a published author, so you might decide to sketch out an outline for a book.

♦ Set yourself a time limit (seriously this time!) for taking that action.

 For example, you might write out your diet plan by the end of the week. Or you might set aside an hour on a specific day or night of the week to work on your book.

. . . .

Even making a plan like this sets the ball rolling.

Take your Life by the Scruff of the Neck

Nothing says *not* enough more than allowing your life to fall into ruin like an untended house, and few things say, 'I *am* enough' more than taking control of your life and satisfying some of your needs and desires. A big part of self-love is taking your life by the scruff of the neck.

So, how about it?

♥♥♥
🏋 **SELF-LOVE GYM:** *Taking Control*

Write down what you are prepared to do in the following areas. I can say that straightening them out has given me a huge boost.

1. Clearing your clutter.

2. Getting control over your finances.

3. Getting meaning and purpose into your life.

4. Being prepared to say 'no'.

5. Straightening out your relationships.

6. Doing stuff you've been putting off.

7. Improving your health.

1) Clearing Your Clutter

Is your bedroom, office, house or garden untidy? Is your life untidy? Your environment reflects your mind. A clutter-free environment reflects an ordered mind.

The goal is to create an environment around you that's nourishing. Clutter is not nourishing. But once you've cleared some of it, you'll be creating space for things that are nourishing. They might include pictures, ornaments, totems, artefacts, new wallpaper... You might even go for a complete overhaul.

To get started, write in the space below what you intend to do and when:

To clear my clutter, I intend to:

_____

And I will aim to do it by: _____

You might notice that I wrote '*aim* to do it by' and not '*will* do it by'. Although I want you to commit to taking some action in your life, I don't want you to beat yourself up if you set the goals but don't find the time to follow them through. Do your best, but go easy on yourself if you don't manage to stick to your plans, because life happens. And you can always come back to them later...

2) Getting Control over Your Finances

If you're in debt, work out a payment plan. Do something, anything, rather than sitting worrying. If you don't know what to do, speak to someone who does. Get their advice and allow them to help you work out some action steps.

If you're good with money, what would it take for you to elevate your financial mastery to the next level?

Make this an important goal, because control over your finances frees up time and energy to do some of the things that matter to you.

> *To get control over my finances, I intend to:*
>
> _____
>
> *And I will aim to do it by:* _____

3) Getting Meaning and Purpose into Your Life

Start by allowing yourself to dream about what it would mean to have purpose in your life. There are two good ways of doing this.

1. The first is to take a piece of paper, set yourself 10 minutes on the clock and just scribble down everything that pops into your mind about what a meaningful life would look like for you.

2. Or you can do it the patient way, by affirming every day that '*Meaning and purpose are flowing into my life.*'

Either way, then sit back and notice what happens. Take particular note of anything unexpected. Unexpected events and chance encounters are often a doorway into something more meaningful, especially if seeking meaning is your goal. Even when the unexpected doesn't seem meaningful at the time, I've found it useful to tell myself, 'OK, let's see where this goes.'

I took two teaching jobs while I was writing my first book, as I mentioned earlier. It was because after my 'enlightened' phase I was financially broke. It seemed a backwards step, as it was reducing the time I had to write, plus I was going back to doing what I'd done at university rather than immersing myself in my new philosophical ideas. But it turned out to be brilliant for me because it gave me vital teaching experience that helped me to refine how I communicated. It also motivated me to structure my writing time better. I finished the book more quickly as a consequence.

When you're looking out for meaning, also pay attention to what friends, family and co-workers say in conversation. You might hear things you've missed in the past because you weren't actively looking for meaning in your life.

To get more meaning and purpose into my life, I intend to:

_____

And I will aim to do it by: _____

4) Being Prepared to Say 'No'

Do you say 'yes' to everyone out of obligation?

Stop it!

Enough said.

5) Straightening Out Your Relationships

Are there problems in any of your relationships that are weighing on your mind? Do you need to have a conversation with anyone? Have you been neglecting any of your relationships? What do you need to do to put this right?

Ask yourself what you need to do to get things on track. Do you need to apologize to anyone? It takes courage and it makes you vulnerable, but the payoff is a clearer mind and it's a big step towards feeling you are enough.

Do you want more passion in any of your relationships? Be the source of it. Don't wait for someone else to bring the topic up in conversation. Plan a romantic dinner. Make more of an effort.

To straighten out my relationships, I intend to:

_____

And I will aim to do it by: _____

6) Doing Stuff You've Been Putting Off

Having a backlog of things to do is psychological clutter (as opposed to physical clutter in your environment; see above). It adds a heavy weight to your mind and leads to a feeling of being out of control. Clearing your backlists, whether it's spending a few days responding to e-mails, tidying the garden, returning phone calls, meeting up with people or having conversations you haven't wanted to have, is highly liberating. You can literally feel the weight lifting off your shoulders.

A simple way to do this is to set aside a whole day or two for it. It's more than worth it. If you work full-time, take a day's holiday. Make it fun. Get excited about it. It will make it much easier.

If you feel you're too busy to make the time, do it anyway. You'll probably find that everything else you do is done more efficiently and effectively because you'll have more energy and your mind will be free to be creative and insightful.

To do stuff I've been putting off, I intend to:

_____

And I will aim to do it by: _____

7) Improving Your Health

What are you prepared to do to take your health by the scruff of the neck? Are you prepared to start exercising more? Can you get up early and go for a jog, do a workout or have a swim? Many successful people have an early morning workout so as to fit staying healthy into their schedule.

What about your dietary habits? What changes are you prepared to make to get healthier?

One of the first things we neglect when we're in not enough consciousness and giving most of our energy to others, is our health. So:

> *To improve my health, I intend to:*

> _____

> *And I will aim to do it by:* _____

Why It's Not Selfish to Look After Your Own Needs

It's admirable being a good friend, parent or Samaritan. The world needs more of them! I passionately believe that a small group of people with compassion and kindness in their hearts can change the world.

But I also believe they will be more effective if they have more energy. And it takes living from 'I *am* enough' to have more energy. *Not* enough is draining. It's emotionally draining, it's mentally draining and it's physically draining. I know because I've lived a lot of my life that way. Adrenaline will only get you so far before you wear yourself out. And self-delusion will only get you so far as well.

What do I mean by 'self-delusion'? I mean the way we tell ourselves that we don't need anything and that giving to others is so spiritually energizing that it supplies all our energy needs. If that actually is true for you, then great. If you can honestly say that you don't sometimes crave a little time for yourself, or a little magic in your life, or control in your life, or just a moment to sit in the sun with a nice glass of wine, then great. It might have been true for Mother Teresa, but I've honestly not come across too many Mother Teresas in my time. And part of 'I *am* enough' is being honest with yourself. It's self-compassionate to do so.

Of course, giving to others *is* spiritually energizing. It's one of *the* most energizing things we can do. I wrote the book on it! In *Why Kindness is Good for You*, I shared the evidence for how kindness benefits us spiritually, emotionally and physically. Giving creates massive amounts of energy. But we still need to breathe! We still need to eat! And we have many other needs, including the need to have some pleasure, happiness, time and magic in our life.

Self-love isn't selfish. As I said right at the beginning, it doesn't mean 'love yourself *instead of* others'. In fact, as we love ourselves more, we have more love to give to others.

Self-love is like an internal bar of soap. It cleans out our heart and mind, leaving plenty of space for compassion and kindness. And that kindness itself is cleaner, fresher, more natural, more honest, more direct, more heartfelt and much more effective.

That's when we become one of that small group of people with compassion and kindness in their hearts who can change the world…

In summary… When we feel we're *not* enough, there's a good chance that we really aren't looking after our own needs that well. We're probably ignoring our wants and needs, in fact.

So, a major step forward is taking control of our life and ensuring those needs and wants are met. Once we take control of our environment, our finances, our relationships and our health and learn how to say 'no' from time to time, we start to feel better, stronger and more balanced, and we say, 'I *am* enough.'

Part IV

Where Are You Going?

'Life shrinks or expands in
proportion to one's courage.'

ANAÏS NIN

Chapter 13

Step Up and Step Out

'If you think something is missing in your life, it's probably YOU.'

ROBERT HOLDEN PHD

You've already taken some action, but now you're building up your self-love it's time to look at really stepping up and achieving what you want in life.

A very important part of self-love is taking action. It's in consistently behaving in a way that says you *are* enough. It usually means pushing yourself out of your comfort zone. To be honest, probably the biggest gains you'll experience in the self-worth stakes will come when you push yourself out of that zone.

Feel the Fear

In *Feel the Fear and Do It Anyway*, Susan Jeffers wrote, 'The "doing it" comes *before* the feeling better about yourself.' If you've been afraid to do things in the past – afraid to have that conversation, afraid to make that phone call, afraid to ask your boss for a rise – and you've been afraid because, deep down, you've felt you were *not* enough, then taking action will boost your feelings of self-worth. But the action comes first!

You'll probably still be scared. Chances are you will be. Everyone gets scared, even the people who do the most posturing and talking themselves up. Most of the time, they're doing that to build up their feelings about themselves because they're just as scared as you are.

Many people want to wait until they've read enough books, been to enough seminars, watched enough interviews and documentaries, grown enough, had that magical or enlightened insight that takes all the fear away. Then it will be easy. That could happen, but not in the way they think.

Overcoming fear doesn't happen by reading books or going on seminars, nor does it happen by sitting at home waiting for the world to come to us. It happens when we step out *into* the world, when we show ourselves as we are. It happens when we step up and step out and say, '*Here I am, world.*'

When we do that, we tell the world, the universe, whatever you want to call it, that we're ready. And when we've done it once, guess what? We do it again, and again, and again! It's consistent action that wires in a sense of being *enough*. Repetition! Repetition! Repetition!

SELF-LOVE GYM: *Remembering Your Courage*

Here's a little exercise to help you to have the courage to step up and step out.

♦ Think back to some times in the past when you were afraid of doing something but did it anyway. What did you do? What was the outcome? How did you feel afterwards? Did it make you feel better about yourself? Write it all down.

For example, I had a fear of public speaking, but I pushed myself to do it and now I really enjoy it. For you, it might be a time when you were afraid to ask a person on a date or for a dance. Or it might have been a risk you took in business. Or it might have been that you were afraid to buy your house. Even if it didn't pan out the way you wanted, you can still include it as an example of having had the courage to do it anyway.

Mind the Gap

I met a guy once who was a talented computer programmer. He was a lovely person and had ideas and dreams that could have morphed into a technology company that could have made a difference to people's lives. Inside, though, he believed he wasn't *enough*. He looked at Mark Zuckerberg and Steve Jobs with great admiration. But he imagined that they had all the know-how that he didn't. He didn't know that they'd started with nothing and had no idea how they were going to realize their dreams.

It's the thought that other people have something you don't that's the problem. It infers you're *not* enough. And it prevents you from acting on your hopes and dreams.

My dream was to be a teacher, covering topics that inspired me. In 1999 I attended an 'Unleash the Power Within' seminar led by Tony Robbins. One of Tony's big teachings was the importance of taking action, especially massive action. So I took massive action. I went back to work the next day and resigned from my job.

OK, I didn't quite think it through, but I'm glad I didn't. I had to work a three-month notice period. I enjoyed that time. I felt free. There was a complete absence of stress in my mind. I was pumped up, dreaming about what I was going to do with my life. I dreamed of writing books, giving talks and leading workshops that would help people to heal and feel good about themselves – exactly what I do now.

I remember waking up with a start early one morning about halfway into my notice period in a sudden panic about what I'd done. I'd resigned from a very good job to be a writer and public speaker. *What?!* First, I'd never been a good writer. It had taken me two attempts to pass my English exam at high school. I was also terrified by speaking in front of people. What had I been thinking?

Sometimes, though, action requires not thinking things through too much. The more we think things through, the more likely we are to come up with reasons why our plans won't work or to become fixated on the problems that might arise. They will arise in fact, because of our feelings of *not* being *enough*. People who live from 'I *am* enough' rarely think things through. They have a dream and they know that somehow they can make it happen.

Some of us aren't so sure, though. A few months after I left that job, I was in the habit of sitting in a little coffee shop in the west end of Glasgow, drinking coffee and reading books. At the time I was reading the *Conversations with God* series written by Neale Donald Walsch. I was also listening to a lot of Wayne Dyer audios in my car. But even though I'd left my job to do what they were doing, when I really thought about it, it seemed above my station. I'd dreamed of doing it. Damn, I'd left my job to do it. But now I was hardly doing anything to move myself in that direction because, deep down, I believed I was *not* enough. It wasn't a conscious belief, more an assumption that coloured my thinking and inhibited meaningful action.

Without meaning to, I was comparing myself to Neale and Wayne. I loved what they were doing. Their words moved me and inspired me in ways I'd never felt before. That was actually part of the problem.

I imagined that anyone who came into contact with Neale or Wayne would have their life changed in about five minutes, such was the wisdom in their words. But I didn't seem to be good at helping people with their problems at all. I had friends who were just as screwed up now as they had been for the previous five years. If I was anything of an influence at all, surely they'd be healed by now. Surely *I'd* be healed by now…

Also, I lacked confidence, despite talking myself up and riding on the whole 'having had the courage to leave my job' thing, and I knew it. Neale and Wayne were obviously super-confident.

Neale and Wayne were also complete, healed, perfect. I wasn't.

I didn't think all this consciously. It was just an assumption about my own worth that led me to imagine there was such a huge gap between me and my heroes and, in my most private moments, to believe in my own deficiencies.

Self-worth lies deep inside. It's a very intimate thing. It's there in our most private thoughts and feelings. It becomes visible in the comparisons we make between ourselves and other people.

I'm sharing my own experience because I've learned that it's much more common than you might think. Everyone compares themselves to others in some way and finds themselves lacking. It might be down to how clever the other people are, how confident, how much money they have, how many resources, how pretty or thin they are, how free of cellulite, how whole... Everyone perceives a gap between themselves and others. But that gap prevents action.

In truth, there *is* no gap. It is artificial. The only place it exists is *inside our own minds*.

Also, as I expect you'll remember, we never really know what's going on in someone else's mind. In all likelihood, the people we're comparing ourselves to have identical fears to us and identical insecurities about their own worth, no matter what they might be doing in the world. We're all human, after all.

I once worked alongside a girl who was beautiful. Everyone thought so. Other girls felt insecure around her. They compared themselves to her and felt they were *not* enough. They saw her as confident. They wished that men would flirt with them as much as they did with her. What they didn't know was that she was just as insecure as they were. The reason she went to such lengths to make herself look attractive was *because* she felt so insecure. Where everybody else saw beauty, she saw only deficiency – something that needed to be improved upon. She felt that she was *not* enough.

There was no gap between how that girl felt and how the others felt. What about you? Do you think there's a gap between you and other people? Is there a gap that prevents you from claiming your worth, from stepping into the world and saying, 'You know what? I *am* enough!'

Once you remove the gap (from your mind), insights come, perceptions change, action is taken and everything changes.

SELF-LOVE GYM: *Removing the Gap*

The mind works in symbolic ways. If you perceive there to be a gap between where you are now and where others are, doing things you'd love to do or being things you'd love to be, imagine building a bridge across it. Make it a nice bridge.

Perhaps you're met on the bridge by people, or even angels, who help you cross. Make it a nice sunny day. Do it as a meditation. Put on some nice music and create a nice setting around yourself.

The symbolic bridging of the gap, and having help to cross, will help you feel better in yourself and more confident that you can get to where you want to go.

Often there are many things that we could do to improve our life, but we don't do them because it never occurs to us that we can. If our root assumption is that we're *not* enough, we'll assume that other people have skills, confidence and self-belief, and we don't. We may put others' success down to money or position. We won't have those either. But great things are often achieved by people who started with nothing – and holding back is almost always down to a feeling of *not* enough.

If you're holding back because of a perceived gap between yourself and others, another way to remove the gap is to start to think of things others do and figure out how you could do them better. It helps reduce the fear of taking action and also helps you realize that you *can* realize your dreams.

 **SELF-LOVE GYM: *Doing It Better***

◆ What are others doing that you could be doing too?

◆ How could you do it better than the other people? What improvements can you identify?

◆ Choose three things and take at least one action step towards each one in the next 48 hours. For example, if others are running online courses and you would like to be doing that too, you could sign up for one of the courses to see how it is done. Or you could talk to someone about getting started.

Interact and Be Kind

As we learned earlier, being authentic creates connections. It's important, then, in stepping up and out into the world, that we interact with people as often as we can in an authentic way. It will help our confidence and also our self-worth.

When we lack self-worth we usually lose confidence and actually shrink away from people. We may make excuses not to interact with them. We may put them down and attempt to elevate ourselves above them. Of course we're only fixating on their deficiencies as a way of plugging our own self-worth deficit.

When we feel good about ourselves, connection is normal. In a state of *enough* there are no blocks to connection.

Turning that around, if we go out and connect, we will start to feel *enough*. So, make a point of interacting with people – shop assistants, waiters, policemen, even the people who issue parking tickets. If you're not used to it, now's the time to get used to it – and good at it. Push yourself out of your comfort zone. It will help you! Even if it feels strange, embarrassing almost, just push through it.

Take an interest in people. And take every opportunity to be kind. Kindness opens hearts. It facilitates vulnerability. It dissolves shame. It shows you for who you really are. It shows that you *are* enough.

And do you know why this is? It's because you *are*.

Leave Your Comfort Zone

In stepping up and out into the world, we find that fear goes away and we can live in happiness and joy. Except ... that isn't quite the way it works. Fear *doesn't* disappear, especially if we continue to challenge and stretch ourselves.

Part of the difficulty a lot of people have with stepping up and out is that they want the fear to go away. Part of the attraction of books about enlightenment, and I know this from personal experience, is the hope that through becoming enlightened we can banish fear. But what if we could change our relationship with it? What if we could just accept it instead? That would mean we'd be more at peace with it, we'd get more used to it and it would lose its grip on us.

We need to make this shift, because in my experience fear never goes away as long as we're consciously stepping up and out. If we can live with that, and expect it, the magic is that fear becomes a friend, something to be expected, welcomed even, because it tells us that what we're about to do matters to us.

So, embrace fear. Step up and out and leave your comfort zone behind. That's a very important part of self-love. *It's not self-love that gets you out there. Getting out there brings you self-love.* Self-love often lies just at the edge of your comfort zone.

Putting in the 'I Am'

And when you step up and out, reflect on the fact that you had the courage and confidence to do it. Don't focus on the problems you overcame. Focus on how you got through those problems.

Focus on what that says about who you are. This is what I call 'putting in the "I am"'.

Confidence comes from '*I have done*', but self-love comes from '*I am.*' So, when you're building up self-love, put in the 'I am'. For example:

♦ 'I faced a fear' means 'I *am* courageous.'

♦ 'I stood up to this person' means 'I *am* learning to stand up for myself.'

♦ 'I spoke publicly' means 'I *am* becoming more confident.'

Bringing your acts of courage and confidence back to yourself in this way will remind you that you are courageous and confident. It will help you face other difficulties and challenges with a sense of meaning, seeing them as opportunities to grow and to develop self-love.

In summary... Action is a hugely important part of self-love. We're always taking action, whether we realize it or not. It's important to act in a way that says, 'I *am* enough.' Often, this involves stepping out of our comfort zone, but happiness, fulfilment and connection usually lie just beyond it.

To reach them, we need to face our fears, but that needn't be something to be afraid of. We can learn to change our relationship to fear by accepting that the goal isn't to get rid of fear but to accept its presence. That's when fear transforms into a friend.

Chapter 14

The Fourth Stage
of Self-Love

*'I have given up the little self for the
Holy Self and I have found the Way.'*

JOHN RANDOLPH PRICE

I was in a room with two men. I seemed to be in some kind of
military service. We knew that an explosion was imminent and
we were about to die. I seemed to believe that I would still exist
afterwards.

Seconds later, the explosion came. I felt warmth. No pain! Just
warmth on my skin. Then I was in a bright white place that was
filled with soft, warm white light. I'm not sure how long I was
there before I noticed that I had no form. I was also aware that I
was on the 'other side' and was a little pleased that even though
my body was gone, I was still alive.

Then I heard a female voice whispering to me. Over and over
again, she whispered, 'Your thoughts create! Your thoughts
create! Your thoughts create!' Then it became 'Your thoughts
create your world! Your thoughts create your world!'

I remember that whisper so clearly. I can hear it now as I write these words.

Then I woke up.

I learned later in the day that my dad's Aunt Lizzie had died that morning. Might my dream somehow have been a communication from her? I thought so. It was one of those dreams that feels so real that when you wake up it takes a few seconds to accept that it was just a dream.

I asked my good friend Kyle Gray about it. He's a highly accurate medium and the bestselling author of *Angel Prayers*.

Kyle asked his angels about my experience. He then told me that because of my sensitive perception, my soul knew Lizzie was passing and it reminded me that, no matter which way we go, we always return to an ever-present love and peace. Lizzie was acknowledging what I'd known all along, so that I'd have a more personal experience of heaven. He said my mind had basically created a scene of going to heaven so I could see that it was all love.

'Wow!' was my response. I trust Kyle and have been on the receiving end of his astonishing otherworldly communication skills on more than one occasion. I believe in what he said. It feels right to me.

Some might think that a scientist has no place talking about life on the other side. I would disagree strongly. I don't subscribe to the idea that consciousness is inside the head, or produced by brain chemistry. Such a notion doesn't account for the wealth of research that shows correlations between the neural states of people separated by a distance. I believe that consciousness is fundamental to reality and that, in a sense, everything is animated by it.

My belief is that just as different shapes, forms, textures and colours of life exist, so different shapes, forms, textures and colours of consciousness exist too, some of which we might interpret or know as angels, guides or deceased loved ones. In some ways, the brain acts like an aerial that tunes to a frequency that extracts from reality what we know as ourselves and others.

Could the consciousness of my dad's aunt have visited me for real? I believe so. I believe that when her brain ceased to function, her consciousness was no longer identified with her physical body. She was then able to be anywhere and she was able to communicate with me.

This leads me into considering a fourth stage of self-love.

A Fourth Stage?

Might there be a kind of fourth stage in the self-love progression from *not* enough to *enough*? OK, 'might there be kind of' isn't the most scientific way I've ever posed a question, but that's because the fourth stage might be construed as spiritual or religious and some might not agree that it even exists.

While many of you will believe in God, spirit, universal consciousness or whatever you choose to call it, many won't. But regardless of spiritual or religious leanings, every one of us needs love to grow. That's a fact of biology and it's also a fact of psychology. And every single person on this planet deserves to know that they are worthwhile, that their very life is relevant. That's also a fact!

So, in the spirit of being authentic, I'd like to present some of my personal views on the nature of existence and why, fundamentally, we all matter.

There's Nothing Inside

It might surprise you to know that the atoms in your body are 99.9999999999999 per cent empty space. That's 13 nines after the decimal point, if you haven't counted. That's like you standing in an empty room that's the size of an average city. It's funny how you're solid, isn't it?

Your atoms are made of subatomic particles: protons, neutrons, electrons, croutons, morons and quarks. (OK, there might be a couple of made-up particles there. I'll leave it to you to guess which.) Particles themselves aren't really made of anything. If you were to prod one, it would feel like the air around a magnet feels when you try to push two of the same poles together – more energy than substance.

Particles emerge out of what's known as the quantum field. It's a field of energy. That's it. There's nothing solid in the quantum field. It's just energy. If you distil down the basic belief in science, we're really all just a bunch of atoms – round about 10 to the power 28, give or take a few. How is it that we can even think?

The conventional assumption is that it's all controlled by brain chemistry. Makes sense! But what if our consciousness or, let's say, our being or essence, is more than the sum of its parts? What if consciousness isn't even inside our head? What if it just feels that way because we have a head? If we didn't have a body, would we still exist?

People who have had near-death experiences (NDEs) would say so. Anita Moorjani experienced being out of her body and watching a resuscitation attempt on it. Her awareness was detached from her body, similar to how mine was in my dream. Her body wasn't at all necessary for her to be conscious.

During her experience she felt her awareness stretch, rather like stretching a rubber band, until she became the entire universe as a state of consciousness. She understood the meaning behind the words 'I am', which many spiritual and religious texts refer to as the name of God.

Anita knew that it was not 'I am *this*' or 'I am *that*' – 'I am a human,' for instance. Anything after 'I am' was smaller than the infinity that she knew herself to be at that moment.

Huge numbers of people have had NDEs. Most just don't speak of them, especially to doctors, in case the doctors believe they have neurological trauma and need to be hospitalized for longer. Would you risk that?

When a doctor is sympathetic, however, and patients feel they can speak freely, the numbers indicate that the experience is surprisingly common. A study by Dutch cardiologist Pim van

Lommel of 344 cardiac patients who had flatlined and been resuscitated found that 62 of them – 18 per cent – had experienced an NDE.[1] Other studies have highlighted a similar statistic.[2]

I won't go into the arguments for and against NDEs because they would fill an entire book and that's not what this book is about. But rather than writing them all off as hallucinations or something else along those lines, could we consider that these experiences are telling us something about the nature of reality?

If it's true that our consciousness is infinite and exists not only outside our brain but throughout the universe, how might it be that we feel ourselves to be human and how does it relate to self-love?

Tuning In

We might think of the brain akin to a Smartphone that's connected to wi-fi, or even a TV. The movie that we watch on our TV set isn't actually inside the television, even though it looks as though it is. Closer inspection of the TV will teach us that the actors are not miniature people inside the set.

The movie is actually buzzing around the atmosphere at close to 186,000 miles (300,000 kilometres) per second. That's about the speed that electromagnetic information is transmitted. The television tunes in to the frequency of the movie and extracts it for us to watch.

If I were to fiddle about with the wires or circuitry in my TV, it would affect the quality of the signal. In a similar way, damage to the brain can affect the signal quality of consciousness. In science, we have stood by a long-held assumption that the fact that damage to the brain affects consciousness means that consciousness is produced by the brain. But the same reasoning would mean that movies are created by the wires and circuit boards in a television set and not simply *received* by the television aerial.

I don't mean to diminish the assumptions made in science. I was trained as a scientist myself. I love science. But science is always evolving. We're always discovering new things and expanding upon the assumptions, theories and experiments of the past.

The idea that consciousness is outside our brain, in fact everywhere in the universe, ties in well with a growing number of experiments that seem to show connectedness between people who are separated by a distance; for instance, studies that use scans of the brain to show that the neural state of one person is correlated with the neural state of another. When one person is stimulated, or even sends a thought by imagining the other person, the neural state of their partner matches theirs.

For example, in a 2004 study 60 individuals were paired into 30 groups and separated in different rooms by approximately 33 feet (10 metres). One person in each pair was asked to send a thought or an image to the other. When they did, the brain of their partner reacted in sync.[3]

In his book *The Sense of Being Stared At*, Rupert Sheldrake, a former fellow and director of studies at Cambridge University and current fellow of the Institute of Noetic Sciences, wrote that when RAF pilots in the Second World War were aiming to shoot down an enemy plane from behind, they were advised not to stare directly at the enemy pilot because the intensity of their stare was known to make them turn around.

Surveys have shown that 70–90 per cent of people say they have sensed someone staring at them from behind,[4] and in one survey 83 per cent of people said that the person they stared at turned around and looked at them.[5] Many CCTV surveillance officers report that people seem to sense when they are being covertly watched.[6]

Have you ever heard your phone ring and immediately got a sense of who it was, then found out you were correct? Sheldrake tested this in a 2009 study. Volunteers between the ages of 11 and 72 offered three phone numbers of friends, colleagues or family members. A computer then randomly selected one of the three numbers and sent the volunteer a text message. They had to guess who it was from. The results were way above statistical chance. The volunteers who scored particularly highly were filmed in an additional experiment and found to guess correctly 44.2 per cent of the time. Chance would have been 33 per cent.[7]

Correlations with Physics

There's an interesting parallel in physics with the idea that consciousness is everywhere.

When a scientist sets up an experiment in a lab to study the behaviour of an electron, until they press the 'on' button and observe the electron it can be thought of as being everywhere in the universe at the same time – including past, present and future. This is known as the Feynman 'sum over histories' (also known as path integral formulation). The late Richard Feynman is considered one of the most highly gifted scientists of all time. He won the Nobel Prize for physics in 1965.

The sum over histories assumes that for a particle like an electron to get from A to B it can take every conceivable path. So, rather than move in a straight line like a ball rolling from one place to another, it can conceivably zig and zag. It can also jump a trillion miles to the left and even zip forwards and backwards in time, do a little jiggly dance and stop off at a little *pâtisserie* in France and enjoy a coffee and an almond croissant before eventually arriving at B.

As ludicrous as that sounds – whoever heard of an electron dancing? – there's nothing in the equations of quantum physics that says it can't happen. In fact, equations that have led to great advancements in science only work out when you make the assumption that until it is observed, a particle is pretty much everywhere.

Does that sound like a description of consciousness?

Consciousness, too, can be thought of as being everywhere until we observe it. Basically that means we – our consciousness, essence, being, etc. – are smeared over the whole universe, past, present and future. Wow! Why doesn't it feel like that?

Well, if you're sitting on a chair right now, chances are you can feel your bottom and you're not listening in to a conversation between two aliens on a distant planet. Detecting sensations in your bottom is called observing, just as detecting electrons in a lab is called observing. And since you're observing your body, you have the sensation of being 'in' your body.

So, consciousness feels as though it's inside our head because we *have* a head and we can feel it, and because we look out through our eyes and listen with our ears. As we do these things, we're observing what we know of as ourselves, just as if we've pressed the 'on' button in a lab.

It's only when we stop observing ourselves, which happens in an NDE or even in a transcendental experience of meditation, that we experience ourselves differently because our attention is not currently on our body. It's so far away from our body that we experience ourselves as infinite.

It can be a difficult concept to get our 'head' around and I can understand why mainstream science is sceptical. We can't prove it one way or the other. We can only rely on experience, and that doesn't hold up too well with the way science is done. But neither does it mean it's wrong!

We're Made of Love

The atoms that make up our body only exist by virtue of the attractive forces that hold them together. If those forces didn't exist then neither would the atoms, just as a cake couldn't exist if we didn't have eggs to bind the ingredients together. If the attractive forces were to be lost at any time, the whole universe as we know it would simply disappear.

You could say there was a law of attraction operating inside atoms. And if that law didn't exist then neither would our body, because atoms make up our DNA, and our DNA combines with other large collections of atoms to make our cells, and our cells join together in an 80-trillion-strong community to form our body.

Here's why, then, I believe we're made of love. The attractive forces emerge out of the quantum field, just as protons do. Science has always assumed that the quantum field is inert, lifeless, partly because of the belief that consciousness is inside the head, but if we move to the idea that consciousness is smeared over the universe and is not inside the head at all, that means it's also smeared all over the quantum field. That's what 'infinite' means – it's everywhere. So it's also in the attractive forces. Consciousness is in the law of attraction.

So, what is the quality of consciousness when one thing, or person, is attracted to another? What is the attractive force? Yes, it's love. We might say that the attractive forces that hold atoms together are quantum expressions of love.

Each of us is made of atoms. That makes us quite a large expression of love. Technically speaking, we're made of love … kind of.

Some spiritual and religious teachings interchange love and light. So we might even say that we're beings of light.

This leads me nicely on to a cool thing that happened while I was working on this book.

The Dove Miracle

I was playing around with the 'being of light' thought for a while and started meditating on the idea that we are all beings of light. I often do a walking meditation when I'm out with Oscar in the early mornings while working on this book, and I'd imagine a being of pure white light materializing right in front of me. Then I'd walk into it as if I was stepping into some clothing, so that I was wearing a being of light suit. For effect, I'd stand up straight, as such a being would, and even flex imaginary angel wings. I'd then combine this with a power pose, or a power walk, which is basically a power pose while walking. I'd state in my mind, 'I am a being of light,' then ask myself, 'How would a being of light walk?' Then I'd walk as a being of light for the next couple of minutes, focusing on my posture, style of movement, face, eyes and breath, all the while imagining myself as pure light and connected with everything and everyone.

I practised this for a few weeks, then went to London to speak at a conference. The day after that I was to speak again in Salzburg, Austria. I'd run out of deodorant and needed to get some so I'd smell fresh for my events. I'd been using the Dove Men's brand for a while, so I left my hotel in search of Dove.

It was starting to rain and I didn't have an umbrella, but suddenly I had an idea. I imagined my being of light suit and stepped into it. (I guess it didn't have a hood, because I still got wet.) I pictured myself as a being of light and connected to the whole city and imagined that the information about where to obtain a Dove deodorant close by would come to me, so I wouldn't get too wet.

My instinct was to turn left at the next street. But on the way, I had the thought that, as a being of light, I really could just stand where I was and hold my hands out and, since I was connected to everything, a Dove Men's deodorant would land in one of them. A being of light would know that it *was* enough and that it was therefore entitled to love, health, happiness, success, wealth and a Dove deodorant. 'As I thinketh, so shall it be,' it would say. That's what was going through my mind as I stood there in the rain.

I didn't test my faith too far though, because the rain was starting to get heavy and, as I said, my being of light suit didn't have a hood. I realized I'd probably have to wait with my hands outstretched for a while and I'd probably get soaked. I did manage to find a shop that sold the brand when I turned left at the next street, though.

But it doesn't end there, because that's really not much of a Dove miracle.

A week later I had another lecture to give in London. My flight from Edinburgh to Heathrow was delayed by four hours, so the staff at British Airways kindly allowed me to transfer to the flight bound for Gatwick.

Arriving at Gatwick meant I needed to take the Gatwick Express train to Victoria station. I wasn't overly familiar with that station, having only been there a handful of times previously. There are also several exits, so it can be a bit confusing if you don't know your way around. Trying to get my bearings, I looked up at the signs to establish where the exits were and which I should take.

Perhaps I should have been paying more attention to looking ahead, though, because I bumped into a young girl and nearly knocked her off her feet.

I instinctively stretched out my hands and said, 'I'm so sorry.'

She looked right at me and then she dropped a Dove Men's deodorant into my hand!

For a few seconds I was stunned. Then the realization of what had just happened hit me. Overcome with that realization, I shouted out, '*Score*!' while pumping the air with my fist.

I'm not sure what the girl thought – maybe that I was rather an excitable chap or even that I'd been travelling for a while and was a bit smelly. Who knows? Several dozen heads turned too, and I'm not sure what they thought either.

I actually keep that deodorant in my pocket as a totem, a reminder of what happened that day. I've not even used it – well, apart from once, when I'd run out of deodorant and was due to speak at a conference the following day. Hmmm, I sense a pattern.

My little Dove Men's deodorant totem reminds me, in my moments of doubt, challenge, worry or fear, of what's possible when we believe.

> **In summary... The fourth stage of self-love is simply 'I am.' So the sequence goes, 'I'm *not* enough', 'I've *had* enough', 'I *am* enough', 'I *am*.'**

Nothing comes after 'I am' because we are infinite. We only feel human now because we have a body. That body exists by virtue of attractive forces in the atoms that are the quantum expression of love. In essence, each of us is a being of light – a physical expression of knowing that it *is*.

Acknowledging we are a being of light affirms that we are more than *enough*, that we *are*.

Would a being of light ever feel unworthy? Would it ever feel it didn't deserve to be happy, to have love in its life, to be successful, to have money, to have a promotion at work, new shoes, a meal at a nice restaurant, some time by itself or a hot bath on a Tuesday? What do you think?

It wouldn't even ask the question. It wouldn't feel either deserving or undeserving. It would just know that if it wanted any of those things then that was fine. It wouldn't have to earn the right to them. It would just be 100 per cent entitled to them. There would be no reason why not.

You are that being of light. Sit with that thought for a moment.

You are entitled to be happy, to have love in your life, to be successful, to have money, a promotion at work, new shoes, a meal at a nice restaurant, some time by yourself or a hot bath on a Tuesday.

So ... go right ahead!

Endnote

Because You're Worth It

'What lies behind us and what lies before us
are tiny compared with what lies within us.'

RALPH WALDO EMERSON

You may have heard the famous L'Oréal slogan 'Because you're worth it.' Those are not empty words. You *are* worth it. You are worthy of love, health, happiness, wealth and all the joys that life has to offer. That's a fact!

So don't be afraid to live your life on your own terms. It's your life. Not someone else's.

Step up! Own your worth. Take responsibility for your life from this moment on. Be a leader in your own life. That's my invitation to you.

Don't make excuses. Don't apologize for being yourself. Don't wait for the world to come to you. Step up and out into the world as yourself. Let the birds sing your name.

Don't be afraid to stretch yourself. Life begins at the edge of your comfort zone.

Live, laugh, love and play! Connect with people. Show them kindness. Be authentic. And always remember to be kind to yourself.

Live your life as you want to live it. It's the only one you have. See how you get on. You've nothing to prove. Who cares if you fall flat on your face? Just get up and have another go.

You don't need to convince anyone of your worth. You're worthy because you are. Your life is worthwhile because it is. The fundamental truth is that you *are* enough. You've never been *not* enough and there will never be a time when you're anything other than *enough*. That is also a fact!

I once saw a poster with the words, 'I am beautiful because…' Do you know the correct ending to that? 'I *am*.'

It's also the beginning!

Afterword

My beloved dog, Oscar, passed away on Wednesday 12 November 2014, aged 2 years and 2 months.

Despite the pain of losing him, I feel deeply blessed for having had him in my life, even for such a short time. Oscar changed me.

I learned to be a parent. He knew me as 'Daddy' and Elizabeth as 'Mummy'.

He arrived in our lives as an 8-week-old puppy around the time I started work on this book, and he passed away around the time I finished it.

Until Oscar came into our lives, I hadn't really stepped up into owning my worth or actually feeling like an adult. I've spoken in the book about how all adults behave like children at times, but deep down I really felt like I hadn't grown up yet, even at the age of 42. Truth be told, I was scared to step up and be an adult. And part of that is parenthood.

Oscar's presence thrust it upon me. Reluctant at first, I found I took to the role very well. It's by far the best 'job' I've ever had.

In the past I had played small a lot, mostly because I was afraid, and because, deep down, I didn't ever feel that I was enough. But because of Oscar, I learned to be an adult instead of hiding. It was a huge self-love thing for me.

Oscar played a massive part in my growth in self-love. I can wholeheartedly say that I would never have been able to write this book without him having been in my life. I believe he came to me to help me, perhaps to save me from myself so that I could move forwards in my life.

Oscar was so loving and playful. I laughed every single day in the 2 years he spent with us. It was impossible to feel unhappy when Oscar was around. He would quickly lift your spirits, taking you out of what you considered to be ever so important. I smile, now, as I think about how he would tell me it was playtime by making a little, almost human, whining noise and sticking his wet nose in my eye socket, or by touching his paw against my face.

Through Oscar I have learned self-love in a way that I didn't know existed. I have learned so much about love in general.

The most powerful demonstration of love I have ever witnessed was when we were going to the vet for Oscar to finally go to sleep. He had a particularly aggressive form of cancer and there was little that we or the vets were able to do to save him. Even after having a leg amputated, the cancer spread into his lungs about three months later. He had contracted kennel cough and the combination was just too much for him.

Despite the deep, all-consuming, gut-wrenching pain of knowing we were about to lose our boy, Elizabeth insisted that we be happy for Oscar. If he sees us sad or afraid it would unsettle him. She wanted his last moments with us to be happy ones. And so they were!

Despite the pain, Elizabeth wasn't concerned for herself. She loved Oscar so much she wanted him to be happy. The experience taught me what real love is about. It taught me about the love in being a parent. It burst me right open, shattering all barriers I had erected between myself and a deeper experience of love.

After he passed, I realized that Oscar had opened my heart so very wide. I had what can only be described as a simmering affection for everyone. I hadn't noticed it before, but once Oscar passed I could feel it almost all the time.

He also gave me the gift of knowing I was worthy of love. He loved me so very much that it was impossible to not accept it.

These are just some of the ways that Oscar's short life changed me. I will forever be grateful for having had the privilege of being his Daddy and I will always cherish the memories of the many, many happy times we shared.

If you want to read a little more about what happened, Elizabeth has dedicated a Facebook page that follows Oscar's last few months. Visit facebook.com/doginterrupted

Notes and References

Chapter 1: The Three Stages of Self-Love

1. B. Grayson and M. I. Stein, 'Attracting assault', *Journal of Communication* 1981, Winter, 31(1), 68–75

Chapter 2: Meet the Parents

1. V. Walkerdine, unpublished study, Department of Psychology, Goldsmiths College, University of London, 1995, cited in Oliver James, *They F*** You Up: How to Survive Family Life*, Bloomsbury, 2002
2. S. S. Luthar and B. E. Becker, 'Privileged but pressured? A study of affluent youth', *Child Development* 2002, 73, 1,593–610
3. Ibid.
4. https://www.youtube.com/watch?v=Yhz3kmXFWrw or simply search 'Oscar Labrador' on YouTube. Video title: 'Oscar, our Labrador puppy, scared to cross the threshold for his first walk.'

Chapter 3: How to Use Your Body to Change How You Feel

1. Dr Cliff Kuhn is a doctor who advocates laughter therapy to improve a person's happiness.
2. C. L. Kleinke, T. R. Peterson and T. R. Rutledge, 'Effects of self-generated facial expressions on mood', *Journal of Personality and Social Psychology* 1998, 74(1), 272–9
3. P. Eckman, 'An argument for basic emotions', *Cognition and Emotion* 1992, 6(3/4), 169–200

4. D. R. Carney, A. J. C. Cuddy and A. J. Yap, 'Power posing: brief nonverbal displays affect neuroendocrine levels and risk tolerance', *Psychological Science* 2010, 21(10), 1,363–8
5. Ibid.
6. Ibid.
7. Ibid.
8. S. Nair, M. Sagar, J. Sollers, N. Consedine and E. Broadbent, 'Do slumped and upright postures affect stress responses? A randomized trial', *Health Psychology* 2014, Sep 15

Chapter 4: Visualization

1. For a summary review, see U. Debamot, M. Sperduti, F. Di Rienzo and A. Guillot, 'Experts' bodies, experts' minds: how physical and mental training shapes the brain', *Frontiers in Human Neuroscience* 2014, 8, article 280, 1–17
2. A. Pascual-Leone, D. Nguyet, L. G. Cohen, J. P. Brasil-Neto, A. Cammarota and M. Hallet, 'Modulation of muscle responses evoked by transcranial magnetic stimulation during the acquisition of new fine motor skills', *Journal of Neurophysiology* 1995, 74(3), 1,037–45, cited in David R. Hamilton, PhD, *How Your Mind Can Heal Your Body*, Hay House, 2008

Chapter 5: Does It Matter If People Like You?

1. J. H. Fowler and N. A. Christakis, 'Dynamic spread of happiness in a large social network: longitudinal analysis over 20 years in the Framingham Heart Study', *British Medical Journal* 2008, 337, a2,338, 1–9

Chapter 7: Body Image

1. A. Furnham and N. Greaves, 'Gender and locus of control correlates of body image dissatisfaction', *European Journal of Personality* 1994, 8, 183–2000
2. V. Cardi, R. Di Matteo, P. Gilbert and J. Treasure, 'Rank perception and self-evaluation in eating disorders', *International Journal of Eating Disorders* 2014, 47(5), 543–52
3. https://www.youtube.com/watch?v=M8JFcim1nkQ or simply search 'Yah! Celebs' eye view' on YouTube.

4. H. G. Pope, K. A. Phillips and R. Olivardia, *The Adonis Complex: The Secret Crisis of Male Body Obsession*, Free Press, 2000

5. T. Moore, 'HIV fears over increase in steroid injections', *Sky News*, 9 April 2014

6. Sarah Grogan, *Body Image*, Routledge, 2008

7. R. Rodgers and H. Chabrol, 'The impact of exposure to images of ideally thin models on body dissatisfaction in young French and Italian women', *Encephale* 2009, 35(3), 262–8

8. I. D. Stephen and A. T-M. Perera, 'Judging the difference between attractiveness and health: does exposure to model images influence the judgments made by men and women?', *PLOS ONE* 2014, 9(1), e86,302

Chapter 10: Self-Compassion

1. Kristin Neff discusses many benefits of self-compassion in *Self-Compassion: Stop Beating Yourself Up and Leave Insecurity Behind*, Hodder, 2011.

2. J. G. Breines, M. V. Thoma, D. Gianferante, L. Hanlin, X. Chen and N. Rohleder, 'Self-compassion as a predictor of interleukin-6 response to acute psychosocial stress', *Brain Behaviour and Immunity* 2014, 37, 109–14

3. T. W. W. Pace, L. T. Negi, D. D. Adame, S. P. Cole, T. I. Sivillia, T. D. Brown, M. J. Issa and C. L. Raison, 'Effect of compassion meditation on neuroendocrine, innate immune and behavioural responses to psychosocial stress', *Psychoneuroendocrinology* 2009, 34(1), 87–98

4. B. Shahar, O. Szesepsenwol, S. Zilcha-Mano, N. Haim, O. Zamir, S. Levi-Yeshuvi and N. Levit-Binnun, 'A wait-list randomized controlled trial of loving-kindness meditation programme for self-criticism', *Clinical Psychology and Psychotherapy* 2014, 16 March, epub ahead of print

5. B. Fredrickson, M. Cohn, K. A. Coffey, J. Pek and S. M. Finkel, 'Open hearts build lives: positive emotions, induced through loving-kindness meditation, build consequential personal resources', *Journal of Personality and Social Psychology* 2008, 95(5), 1,045–62

6. P. Pearsall, 'Contextual cardiology: what modern medicine can learn from ancient Hawaiian wisdom', *Cleveland Clinical Journal of Medicine* 2007, 74(1), S99–104. The research this

paper described as an example of 'Hard Marriage, Hard Heart' was: T. W. Smith, C. Berg, B. N. Uchino, P. Florsheim and G. Pearce, 'Marital conflict behavior and coronary artery calcification', paper presented at the American Psychosomatic Society's 64th Annual Meeting, Denver, CO, 3 March 2006

7. C. A. Hutcherson, E. M. Seppala and J. J. Gross, 'Loving-kindness meditation increases social connectedness', *Emotion* 2008, 8(5), 720–24

8. J. W. Carson, F. J. Keefe, T. R. Lynch, K. M. Carson, V. Goli, A-M. Fras and S. R. Thorp, 'Loving-kindness meditation for chronic low back pain', *Journal of Holistic Nursing* 2005, 23(3), 287–304

9. P. Arnstein, M. Vidal, C. Wells-Federman, B. Morgan and M. Caudill, 'From chronic pain patient to peer: benefits and risks of volunteering', *Pain Management Nursing* 2002, 3(3), 94–103

Chapter 11: Forgiveness

1. See Chapter 12: 'Letting Go of the Past' in David R. Hamilton, PhD, *Why Kindness is Good for You*, Hay House, 2010. The individual references cited there are: R. D. Enright, E. A. Gassin and C. Wu, 'Forgiveness: a developmental view', *Journal of Moral Education* 1992, 21, 99–114; C. V. O. Witvliet, T. E. Ludwig and K. L. Vander Laan, 'Granting forgiveness or harbouring grudges: implications for emotion, physiology, and health', *Psychological Science* 2001, 121, 117–23; J. P. Friedberg, S. Suchday and D. V. Shelov, 'The impact of forgiveness on cardiovascular reactivity and recovery', *International Journal of Psychophysiology* 2007, 65(2), 87–94; M. Waltman, D. Russell and R. Enright, 'Research study suggests forgiving attitude may be beneficial to the heart', paper presented at the American Psychosomatic Society Annual Meeting, 5–8 March 2003, Phoenix, Arizona; D. Tibbits, G. Ellis, C. Piramelli, F. M. Luskin and R. Lukman, 'Hypertension reduction through forgiveness training', *Journal of Pastoral Care and Counselling* 2006, 60(1–2), 27–34; M. E. McCulloch, L. M. Root and A. D. Cohen, 'Writing about the benefits of an interpersonal transgression facilitates forgiveness', *Journal of Consulting and Clinical Psychology* 2006, 74(5), 887–97

Chapter 14: The Fourth Stage of Self-Love

1. P. van Lommel, R. van Wees, V. Meyers and I. Elfferich, 'Near death experience in survivors of cardiac arrest: a prospective study in the Netherlands', *The Lancet* 2001, 358, 2,039–45

2. See http://en.wikipedia.org/wiki/Near-death_experience

3. L. J. Standish, L. Kozac, L. C. Johnson and T. Richards, 'Electroencephalographic evidence of correlated event-related signals between the brains of spatially and sensory isolated human subjects', *Journal of Alternative and Complementary Medicine* 2004, 10(2), 307–14

4. Cited in R. Sheldrake, *Seven Experiments That Could Change the World: A Do-It-Yourself Guide to Revolutionary Science*, Fourth Estate, 1994

5. Cited in R. Sheldrake, *The Sense of Being Stared At*, Century Hutchinson, 2003

6. Ibid.

7. R. Sheldrake, L. Avraamides and M. Novak, 'Sensing the sending of SMS messages: an automated test', *Explore* 2009, 5(5), 272–6

ABOUT THE AUTHOR

Photographer: Stephen Mulhearn

David R. Hamilton gained a first-class honours degree in chemistry, specializing in biological and medical chemistry, and a PhD in organic chemistry. After graduating in 1995, David spent four years working for one of the world's largest pharmaceutical companies, and also served as an athletics coach and team manager for one of the UK's top athletics clubs. He left both roles in 1999. In 2000 he co-founded Spirit Aid Foundation, an international relief charity helping children whose lives have been affected by war and poverty. In 2002, as a director of Spirit Aid, he helped produce a 9-day, 24-event festival of peace in Glasgow. He served as a director of Spirit Aid until the end of 2002. From 2004 until 2005, he taught chemistry and ecology at James Watt College of Further and Higher Education, and tutored chemistry at the University of Glasgow.

In 2005, he self-published his first book, *It's the Thought That Counts*, which was published by Hay House in 2006. David is now the author of eight books, all published by Hay House. He has been featured on TV and radio and been the subject of numerous national newspaper articles. He spends most of his time writing, giving talks, and leading workshops. David also writes a regular blog for *Psychologies* magazine and *The Huffington Post*.

www.drdavidhamilton.com

HAY HOUSE

Look within

Join the conversation about latest products,
events, exclusive offers and more.

f Hay House

🐦 @HayHouseUK

📷 @hayhouseuk

♥ healyourlife.com

We'd love to hear from you!